Colombia

Peace and Stability in the Post-Conflict Era

AUTHORS
Carl Meacham
Douglas Farah
Robert D. Lamb

A Report of the CSIS Americas Program

March 2014

CSIS | CENTER FOR STRATEGIC & INTERNATIONAL STUDIES

ROWMAN & LITTLEFIELD
Lanham • Boulder • New York • Toronto • Plymouth, UK

About CSIS

For over 50 years, the Center for Strategic and International Studies (CSIS) has developed solutions to the world's greatest policy challenges. As we celebrate this milestone, CSIS scholars are developing strategic insights and bipartisan policy solutions to help decisionmakers chart a course toward a better world.

CSIS is a nonprofit organization headquartered in Washington, D.C. The Center's 220 full-time staff and large network of affiliated scholars conduct research and analysis and develop policy initiatives that look into the future and anticipate change.

Founded at the height of the Cold War by David M. Abshire and Admiral Arleigh Burke, CSIS was dedicated to finding ways to sustain American prominence and prosperity as a force for good in the world. Since 1962, CSIS has become one of the world's preeminent international institutions focused on defense and security; regional stability; and transnational challenges ranging from energy and climate to global health and economic integration.

Former U.S. senator Sam Nunn has chaired the CSIS Board of Trustees since 1999. Former deputy secretary of defense John J. Hamre became the Center's president and chief executive officer in April 2000.

CSIS does not take specific policy positions; accordingly, all views expressed herein should be understood to be solely those of the author(s).

ISBN: 978-1-4422-2811-5 (pb); 978-1-4422-2812-2 (eBook)

Center for Strategic & International Studies
1616 Rhode Island Avenue, NW
Washington, DC 20036
202-887-0200 | www.csis.org

Rowman & Littlefield
4501 Forbes Boulevard
Lanham, MD 20706
301-459-3366 | www.rowman.com

Contents

Executive Summary

The project that culminated in this report was conceived just over a year ago as an initiative to assess the major accomplishments in strengthening the Colombian government's efforts to bring peace and stability to its countryside.

The project's primary goal was to examine what the government of Colombia is currently doing to consolidate the success it has achieved and prevent any regression to the problems that have long plagued the country—with a particular focus on the role of U.S. policy given the place of the United States as Colombia's key regional security partner.

Overall, this project sought to determine whether the United States is on the right course in reducing security and in development assistance to Colombia by the 2014 deadline. The project sought to identify those areas where continued support is still necessary and most pivotal—and where it can most effectively foster the consolidation of the gains achieved to date.

In this task, the project could then become a point of reference for U.S. policymakers in determining the future course of the countries' bilateral relationship. At a time when political discourse in Washington is polarized and discretionary spending is tight, the project aimed to provide unique insights into Colombia and the unfolding situation there, as well as to offer policy options that would have broad, bipartisan appeal in the United States.

At the time of publication, the Colombian government and the Revolutionary Armed Forces of Colombia (FARC)—the armed political insurgency largely responsible for the widespread rural violence that has plagued the country for decades—were engaged in negotiations seeking to end Colombia's decades-long conflict. Though the talks' prospects are themselves uncertain, the peace process is currently the way forward agreed upon by both sides in the conflict—and an important alternative for consolidating its hard-earned gains and finally bringing an end to the 50 years of fighting that have left in their wake hundreds of thousands of casualties and immeasurable human suffering.

To be sure, countless factors play into the achievement and consolidation of a real and lasting peace in Colombia. The peace process, the upcoming electoral cycle, and the political and economic stability of Venezuela—each of these has the potential to secure (or prevent) the resolution of the decades-long conflict. These variables remain in a constant state of flux, and the country is at a critical juncture. Colombia's very future—all that the country has worked to achieve—hangs in the balance.

By means of this report, we hope to take up this issue, addressing where Colombia stands now, how it has gotten there, and where it will be moving forward. Ultimately our recommendations, which will be elaborated on later in the executive summary, are as follows:

1. The U.S.-Colombia strategic partnership should continue for the foreseeable future—even if the ongoing peace process proves successful in formally ending the principal conflict and resolving the several outstanding issues on its agenda.

2. In that vein, the following issues will likely emerge as central to the two countries' partnership in the future: land restitution; offensive action against nonguerrilla perpetrators of violence; support for the Colombian judiciary; resource allocation for internally displaced persons; protection for the country's indigenous communities and other vulnerable groups; and the clearing of nonstate armed actors from areas of illicit resource extraction.

3. It is also imperative that the Colombian government take on a number of initiatives of its own, including: an effective public messaging campaign to alter continued perceptions that the country remains at war; and a monitoring and evaluation framework, to keep track of whether and to what extent progress is being made in the consolidation programs already in place.

Colombia Then and Now

Colombian president Juan Manuel Santos and his government spent the summer and fall engaged in peace talks with the FARC, with an eye to ending the widespread rural violence that has plagued the country for decades. And while the talks' prospects have fluctuated with the unpredictable behavior of Venezuelan leadership—a key player in the ongoing conflict and negotiations—it cannot be denied that, whatever the talks' outcome, the Colombian government has made huge strides in ameliorating the struggles the country has faced over the course of the last decade.

Much of that progress is credited to Colombia's own efforts—but important, as well, are the results obtained through Plan Colombia, a bilateral effort of the Colombian and U.S. governments begun in 2000 to address the South American country's challenges and strengthen the Colombian government's ability to establish peace, law, and order in its national territory.

By most accounts, in 2000 the government was barely in control of one-third of Colombia's countryside and had ceded a sanctuary the size of Switzerland to terrorist insurgents. Just seven years later, government presence had extended into about 90 percent of national territory, and in 2008 security forces rescued 15 high-profile hostages and decimated the insurgency's leadership in a series of successful raids.

A 2008 the U.S. Government Accountability Office (GAO) report stated that Plan Colombia—and the U.S. aid included in it—had helped cut Colombia's homicide rate nearly in half. At the same time, annual kidnappings were reduced by over 85 percent.[1] And the use of the country's highways increased by nearly 60 percent in the first six years of the partnership alone, a signal of the population's growing confidence in the security of the roads and the countryside they traverse.

In recent years Colombia has begun to enjoy the major security gains derived both through its own efforts and by means of Plan Colombia. And though there is still much work to be done, as the country has become an increasingly stable partner, the U.S.-Colombia relationship has begun to shift in kind.

Once focused on U.S. aid for Colombian efforts to improve the rule of law, effect stability, and root out rural violence, the two countries have now turned to an increasingly commercial phase in their relations, with the U.S.-Colombia Trade Promotion Agreement (CTPA) and a sharp increase in U.S. foreign direct investment (FDI) in recent years; from 2010 to 2011, U.S. FDI in Colombia increased by 7 percent,[2] and from 2011 to 2012, FDI increased by an additional 15 percent.[3]

By most measures, then, the U.S.-Colombia partnership ranks among the most successful of its kind. It would, however, be a grave mistake to assume that the work is done. Though Colombia remains among the top 10 recipients of U.S. military assistance, the United States is drawing down bilateral aid as part of its exit strategy to end the Plan Colombia partnership by 2014.

With the United States focused on the expanding commercial side of the relationship, there are concerns that it may be too soon to draw down bilateral security, counternarcotic, and development efforts when state authority has yet to be permanently extended to broad swaths of Colombia's countryside. Despite impressive progress, reduced guerilla fronts continue to operate, and some demobilized insurgent and paramilitary combatants have returned to murder, marauding, and drug trafficking.

If Colombia's many gains are not consolidated, its recently hard-won progress could recede, propelling the countryside back into the hands of transnational criminals and terrorists.

New Hope: The Peace Process

After decades of conflict and a dozen years of efforts under Plan Colombia, the Colombian government agreed to begin long-awaited talks with the FARC in November 2012, marking the first time the two parties to the conflict had attempted negotiations since 2002. Six

1. U.S. Government Accountability Office (GAO), "GAO-09-71: Plan Colombia," October 6, 2008, http://www.gao.gov/assets/290/282511.pdf.
2. "Colombia," Office of the U.S. Trade Representative, 2012, http://www.ustr.gov/countries-regions/americas/colombia.
3. "Preliminary Overview of Latin America and the Caribbean: Colombia," Economic Commission for Latin America and the Caribbean, 2013, http://www.eclac.org/publicaciones/xml/ 3/48593/Colombia_ing.pdf.

months later, the two groups reached an agreement on the first of the six issues on the agenda: rural land reform.

Early this fall, with just over four months remaining before the hoped-for deadline of January 2014, the FARC officially put the negotiations process on hold. But just a few weeks after the start of this "pause," the two sides resumed talks, quickly coming to an agreement on the second issue on the agenda: the political participation of the FARC.

The pause, which was requested after the government announced its hopes for a public referendum on whatever agreement is derived from the talks during the national election cycles next year, was met with mixed reactions.

On one hand, there were those—including the government negotiators—who voiced their understanding of the FARC's break, citing the group's need to consider the referendum proposal and its effects, particularly given their preference for a constituent assembly that could engrain the accords in Colombia's constitution. And, in the context of the breakthrough achieved in May and the various statements made by both sides as to their firm intention to see the process through and effect a real and lasting peace, the pause, so the argument goes, paled in comparison to the progress made in the lead-up to it.

That said, many still fear that the pause was another on a long list of delays and obstacles that collectively may stand in the way of successful negotiations. With the initial deadline fast approaching and four major agenda items still to be addressed, the pressure is on both the government and the FARC to ensure an expedient and—to the extent possible—meaningful process. The worry, then, is that this delay may be the straw that broke the proverbial camel's back, even with the talks back up and running.

Even such worries, though, were largely dispelled by the quick resumption of the talks—and the even quicker resolution of the issue of political participation, considered one of the most controversial aspects of the negotiations.

The hope, then, is that the two sides will use the momentum they have built to address the remaining agenda items and proceed through the entire framework for peace.

The coming electoral cycle adds still another dimension of complexity to the negotiations, as well. Colombian president Juan Manuel Santos's hope to ratify the agreement in a public referendum during the national elections in early 2014 puts additional pressure on the process—the accords can be put to a public vote only if they have been concluded well in advance of election day. And because of the January deadline for the peace process—a deadline set by President Santos—the government faces pressure to conclude the negotiations on time. A failure to do so would likely factor into their reelection prospects.

The Report: Colombia: Peace and Stability in the Postconflict Era

Ultimately, this report's findings should be useful for both the United States and Colombia. The latter case may be more straightforward. After all, it can hardly be argued that an in-depth look at the effects of decreased U.S. aid to Colombia are anything but pivotal to the South American country's consolidation of the gains it has worked so hard to earn. But the findings are no less valuable for the United States.

At its inception, Plan Colombia was the largest expenditure in the U.S. foreign aid budget outside of Israel and Egypt. The bilateral security partnership model it followed is one characteristic of U.S. efforts around the world—and failure of the partnership could imply the parallel failure of all U.S. partnerships built along the same model. Such a failure would suggest that the billions of dollars in aid the U.S. government has contributed to the efforts toward Colombia's peace and stability were ultimately wasted on an unachievable—or at least as-yet unachieved—goal. Plan Colombia's success or failure, then, represents an evaluation of U.S. regional foreign policy since 2000.

This project set out to evaluate five critical areas, which mirror the key points of President Santos's development plan:

1. Distribution of people, resources, and infrastructure
2. Effectiveness of public security and the extent of state authority
3. Development of economic opportunity
4. Social integration of rural populations
5. Role and effectiveness of current U.S. security and development assistance.

Through an in-depth analysis of these areas, this project sought to answer a pair of central questions:

1. To what extent have joint U.S.-Colombian efforts succeeded in ending the violence that has plagued the country for a half-century?
2. What should be the role of the United States moving forward in Colombia's efforts to consolidate its gains and effect real and lasting peace throughout its national territory?

What follows is the full explanation of the project's findings.

Recommendations and Conclusions

Given this report's exploration of the current state of Colombia's ongoing conflict and the challenges the government and country will continue to face going forward, the authors propose the following recommendations:

1. The U.S.-Colombia strategic partnership should continue for the foreseeable future—even if the ongoing peace process proves successful in formally ending the principal conflict and resolving the several outstanding issues on its agenda.

    - The political implications of losing influence in Colombia would be significant. Damage to that relationship could include the loss of a key ally who has consistently demonstrated support for policies key to U.S. interests—both in the region and around the world.

    - But furthering their cooperation, the U.S. and Colombian governments must become flexible and agile in dealing with the shifting security challenges the two will face as Colombia moves forward.

    - The recent shifts in the nature of the conflict are largely a reflection of the success of the joint strategy of dismantling the major existential threats to the state. But maintaining the current positive trends will require a constant reevaluation of the national strategy and goals, as well as of resource allocation.

2. In that vein, the following issues will likely emerge as central to the two countries' partnership in the future: land restitution; offensive action against nonguerrilla perpetrators of violence; support for the Colombian judiciary; resource allocation for internally displaced persons; protection for the country's indigenous communities and other vulnerable groups; and the clearing of nonstate armed actors from areas of illicit resource extraction.

    - *Land Restitution:* The issue of land restitution must remain among the top priorities of the partnership. The recent progress has given the government some breathing room, with an opportunity to establish a positive state presence. Still, the issue has the real potential to develop into a fatal bottleneck. Land disputes deeply affect the Colombian population and are often a primary driver of rural violence. Efforts to resolve this complex and thorny problem must be accelerated, and U.S. aid in this field should ideally focus on providing technological support to these efforts. Although at best the horizon for measuring success remains several years off, the more robust the effort, the more credible the overall strategy becomes.

    - *Nonguerrilla Perpetrators of Violence:* Should the conflict with armed guerrilla forces wind down, the greatest threat to both social inclusion and government consolidation will likely be the continued impunity of the powerful, nonguerrilla landholders whose private security details continue to threaten and attack vulnerable minorities, internally displaced persons (IDPs), and recently victims who have returned to their land. Whether these groups are referred to as demobilized paramilitaries, BACRIM, or simply power brokers protecting their perceived interests, their continued impunity demonstrates that the state does not have a monopoly on violence—even despite the departure of guerrillas. It also suggests that the state is unwilling, and/or unable, to live up to its promises to treat excluded and vulnerable persons as citizens worthy of state protection. Moving forward, the

Colombian government needs to build its capacity to pursue, investigate, prosecute, and (if necessary) do battle against those who continue to perpetrate violence.

- *The Colombian Judiciary:* The judiciary has, without a doubt, come a long way since the 1990s. That said, the courts continue to suffer from understaffing. This renders them incapable of keeping up with the need to prosecute perpetrators of crimes and with the demand for specialized legal services as land and property rights issues emerge and develop. Support for paralegal training and scholarships for law school students might be useful steps in addressing these issues in the medium term, building judicial capacity to benefit the country in coming years.
- *Internally Displaced Persons (IDPs):* The deficiency of resources for IDPs continues to hamper the process of reintegrating these people into their communities of origin. Regional IDP centers should be set up in more remote areas—perhaps in tandem with other government offices—so that IDPs need not travel long distances to register for and receive the services provided for them. The U.S. and Colombian governments should work together to institutionalize the changes that have already been made and ensure that the institutions and personnel that work to better this issue are adequately trained and financially supported.
- *Indigenous and Vulnerable Groups:* Indigenous communities and other vulnerable groups—among them women and Afro-Colombians—remain disproportionately affected by the conflict and its implications, and by the violence and land expropriation in particular. Many Afro-Colombian and indigenous communities, especially those seeking to preserve their ways of life, remain too poor to adequately represent themselves before the courts or protect themselves from all sides of the conflict. Every effort should be made to ensure the protection of their traditional lands, ensuring that title to their lands is not improperly awarded to other claimants—and to provide legal services and other forms of support to improve their access to the judicial system.
- *Illicit Resource Extraction:* As a military priority, efforts should focus on the clearing of nonstate armed actors from areas of illicit extraction of minerals and other resources. The ability of these groups to access and sell coltan, gold, emeralds, and other minerals both deprives the state of revenue and has served as an economic lifeline for irregular groups that feed into the nation's violence. Illegal mining—when carried out by such armed groups—offers a stream of revenue to these actors and implies few of the risks of being involved in the production and trade of cocaine. The issue must be addressed if the groups are to be deprived of the financial resources they need to continue their operations.

3. It is also imperative that the Colombian government take on a number of initiatives of its own, including: an effective public messaging campaign to alter continued perceptions that the country remains at war; and a monitoring and evaluation framework, to keep track of whether and to what extent progress is being made in the consolidation programs already in place.

1 Introduction

By Carl Meacham

At the time of publication, negotiations had resumed between the Colombian government and the Revolutionary Armed Forces of Colombia (FARC), the armed political insurgency largely responsible for the widespread rural violence that has plagued the country for decades. Though the talks' prospects are themselves uncertain, the peace process is currently the way forward agreed upon by both sides in the conflict—and an important alternative for consolidating its hard-earned gains and finally bringing an end to the 50 years of fighting that have left hundreds of thousands of casualties and immeasurable human suffering in their wake.

To be sure, countless factors play into the achievement and consolidation of a real and lasting peace in Colombia. The peace process, the upcoming electoral cycle, and the political and economic stability of Venezuela—each of these has the potential to secure (or prevent) the resolution of the decades-long conflict. Even as these variables remain in a constant state of flux, the country is at a critical juncture. Colombia's very future—all that the country has worked to achieve—hangs in the balance.

By means of this report, we hope to take up this issue, addressing where Colombia stands now, how it has gotten there, and where it may go moving forward.

Colombia Then and Now

Colombian president Juan Manuel Santos and his government spent the summer engaged in peace talks with the FARC, with an eye to ending the widespread rural violence that has plagued the country for decades. And although the talks' prospects have fluctuated with the unpredictable behavior of Venezuelan leadership—a key player in the ongoing conflict and negotiations—it cannot be denied that, whatever their outcome, over the course of the last decade the Colombian government has made huge strides in ameliorating the struggles the country faces.

Much of that progress is credited to Colombia's own efforts, but also to the results obtained through Plan Colombia, a bilateral effort of the Colombian and U.S. governments begun in 2000 to address the South American country's challenges and strengthen the Colombian government's ability to establish peace, law, and order in its national territory.

By most accounts, in 2000 the government was barely in control of one-third of Colombia's countryside and had ceded a sanctuary the size of Switzerland to terrorist insurgents. Just seven years later, government presence had extended into about 90 percent of national territory, and in 2008 security forces rescued 15 high-profile hostages and destroyed much of the insurgency's leadership in a series of successful raids.

The U.S. Government Accountability Office reported that Plan Colombia—and the U.S. aid included in it—helped cut Colombia's homicide rate nearly in half. At the same time, annual kidnappings were reduced by over 85 percent.[1] And the use of the country's highways increased by nearly 60 percent in the first six years of the partnership—a signal of the population's growing confidence in the security of the roads and the countryside they traverse.

In recent years Colombia has begun to enjoy the major security gains derived both through its own efforts and via Plan Colombia. Although there is still much work to be done, as the country has become an increasingly stable partner, the U.S.-Colombian relationship has begun to shift in kind. Once focused on U.S. aid for Colombian efforts to improve the rule of law, affect stability, and root out rural violence, the two countries have now turned to an increasingly commercial phase in their relations, with the U.S.-Colombia Free Trade Agreement and a sharp increase in U.S. foreign direct investment (FDI) in recent years; from 2010 to 2011, U.S. FDI in Colombia increased by 7 percent,[2] and from 2011 to 2012, FDI increased by an additional 15 percent.[3]

By most measures, then, the U.S.-Colombian partnership ranks among the most successful of its kind. It would, however, be a grave mistake to assume that the work is done. Though Colombia remains among the top 10 recipients of U.S. military assistance, the United States is drawing down bilateral assistance as part of its exit strategy to end the Plan Colombia partnership by 2014.

With the United States focused on the expanding commercial side of the relationship, there are concerns that it may be too soon to end bilateral security, counternarcotic, and development efforts when state authority has yet to be permanently extended to broad swaths of Colombia's countryside. Despite impressive progress, reduced guerilla fronts continue to operate, and some demobilized insurgent and paramilitary combatants have returned to murder, marauding, and drug trafficking. If Colombia's many gains are not consolidated, its recently hard-won progress could recede, propelling the country back into the hands of transnational criminals and terrorists.

---

1. U.S. Government Accountability Office, "GAO-09-071: Plan Colombia," October 6, 2008, http://www.gao.gov/assets/290/282511.pdf.
2. Office of the U.S. Trade Representative (USTR), "Colombia," 2012, http://www.ustr.gov/countries-regions/americas/colombia.
3. Economic Commission for Latin America and the Caribbean (ECLAC), "Colombia," 2013, http://www.eclac.org/publicaciones/xml/3/48593/Colombia_ing.pdf.

New Hope: The Peace Process

After decades of conflict and a dozen years of efforts under Plan Colombia, the Colombian government agreed to begin long-awaited talks with the FARC in November 2012, marking the first time the two parties to the conflict had attempted negotiations since 2002. Six months later, the two groups reached an agreement on the first of the six issues on the agenda: rural land reform. Early this fall, with just over four months remaining before the hoped-for deadline of January 2014, the FARC officially put the negotiations process on hold. But just a few weeks after the start of this "pause," the two sides resumed talks, quickly coming to an agreement on the second issue on the agenda: the political participation of the FARC.

The pause, which was requested after the government's announcement of its hopes for a public referendum on whatever agreement is derived from the talks during the national election cycles next year, was met with mixed reactions. On one hand, there were those—including the government negotiators—who voiced their understanding of the FARC's break, citing the group's need to consider the referendum proposal and its effects, particularly given their preference for a constituent assembly that could engrain the accords in the country's constitution. And in the context of the breakthrough achieved in May and the various statements made by both sides as to their firm intention to see the process through and effect a real and lasting peace, the pause, so the argument goes, paled in comparison to the progress made in the lead-up to it.

That said, many fear that the pause was another on a long list of delays and obstacles that collectively may stand in the way of successful negotiations. With the initial deadline fast approaching and four major agenda items still to be addressed, the pressure is on both the government and the FARC to ensure an expedient and—to the extent that it is possible—amicable process. The worry, then, is that this delay may be the straw that broke the proverbial camel's back—even with the talks back up and running. Even such worries, though, were largely dispelled by the quick resumption of the talks—and the even quicker resolution of the issue of political participation, considered one of the most controversial aspects of the negotiations. The hope, then, is that the two sides will use the momentum they have built to address the remaining agenda items and proceed through the entire framework for peace.

The coming electoral cycle adds still another dimension of complexity to the negotiations. Colombian President Juan Manuel Santos's hope to ratify the agreement in a public referendum during the national elections in early 2014 puts additional pressure on the process—the accords can be put to a public vote only if they have been concluded well in advance of election day. And because of the January deadline for the peace process—a deadline set by President Santos—the government faces pressure to conclude the negotiations on time. A failure to do so would likely factor into their reelection prospects.

La Otra Colombia: The CSIS Americas Program and Colombian Security

The project that would culminate in this report was initially conceived just over a year ago as an initiative to assess the major accomplishments in strengthening Colombia's efforts to bring peace and stability to its countryside. The project's primary goal was to examine what Colombia is currently doing to consolidate the success it has achieved and to prevent a recurrence of the problems that have long plagued the country—with a particular focus on the role of the United States moving forward, given its place as Colombia's key security partner.

Overall, this project sought to determine whether the United States is on the right course in reducing security and development assistance to Colombia by the 2014 deadline. The project sought to identify those areas where continued support is still necessary and most pivotal—and where it can most effectively foster the consolidation of the gains achieved to date.

In this task the project could then become a point of reference for U.S. policymakers in determining the future course of the countries' bilateral relationship. At a time when political discourse in Washington is polarized and discretionary spending is tight, the project aimed to provide unique insights into Colombia and the unfolding situation there, as well as offer policy options that would have broad appeal.

The Report: Colombia East and West of the Andes

Ultimately this report's findings should be useful for both the United States and Colombia. The latter case may be more straightforward. After all, it can hardly be argued that an in-depth look at the effects of decreased U.S. aid to Colombia are anything but pivotal to the South American country's consolidation of the gains it has worked so hard to earn. But the findings are no less valuable for the United States.

At its inception, Plan Colombia was the largest expenditure in the U.S. foreign aid budget outside of Israel and Egypt. The bilateral security partnership model it followed is one characteristic of U.S. efforts around the world—and failure of the partnerships would imply the parallel failure of all U.S. partnerships built along the same model. Such a failure would suggest that the billions of dollars in aid the U.S. government has contributed to the efforts toward peace were ultimately wasted on an unachievable—or at least as yet unachieved—goal. The implications for the United States of Plan Colombia's success or failure, then, are countless.

This project set out to evaluate five critical areas, which mirror the key points of President Santos's development plan:

1. The distribution of people, resources, and infrastructure
2. The effectiveness of public security and the extent of state authority

3. The development of economic opportunity
4. The social integration of rural populations
5. The role and effectiveness of current U.S. security and development assistance

Through an in-depth analysis of these areas, this project sought to answer a pair of central questions:

1. To what extent have joint U.S.-Colombian efforts succeeded in ending the violence that has plagued the country for a half-century?
2. What should be the role of the United States moving forward in Colombia's efforts to consolidate its hard-earned gains and effect real and lasting peace throughout its national territory?

What follows is the full explanation of the project's findings. Before launching into the bulk of the report's analysis, we turn first to a brief history of Colombia's rural conflict, beginning with its roots in the 1920s and continuing through the current Santos administration. In the chapters that follow, the report addresses the issues most central to the country's long conflict: security, land tenure, natural resources, infrastructure, governance, and social inclusion. The report concludes with a set of recommendations for Colombia and the U.S.-Colombia partnership moving forward, in the context of all that has happened in recent years.

2 History of Rural Conflict

By Carl Meacham

Overview

The ongoing rural conflict in Colombia has plagued the country for decades. Three main factors have contributed to its nature and persistence: a lack of effective government policies and state presence in rural areas; the creation of guerilla and paramilitary groups; and the emergence of drug-trafficking organizations. Together, these three factors have made Colombia's rural history one characterized by violence and poverty. With millions of people displaced, thousands killed and kidnapped, and the strong presence of illegal armed groups in rural areas, the development of Colombia's countryside is a challenge that remains to be met.

To date, the Colombian government has made progress in developing national security policies that have helped reduce crime and violence in the countryside. With strategic projects—such as Plan Colombia, Plan of Democratic Security, Sword of Honor Campaign, Green Heart Plan, and National Consolidation Plan—the country has witnessed substantial improvement in security. The situation in the rural sector has dramatically changed. As the state's presence in rural areas has increased, the role of drug trafficking has diminished, paramilitary groups have been partially disarmed, and the government and the guerillas have engaged in (ongoing) peace negotiations. With these security measures, the government has made Colombia more favorable for investment and has implemented policies to boost socioeconomic development in rural areas.

Part I: Beginning of Rural Conflict and Rural Violence

The roots of the current rural conflict in Colombia can be traced back to the 1920s. The Great Depression hit the Colombian economy hard, and as unemployment increased in urban areas, many Colombians migrated to coffee plantations—at that point the staple of the country's economy—in the countryside. But as the international demand for coffee increased, so did plantations' land values. The government viewed the increase in coffee demand as an opportunity to appropriate land and sell it to wealthy entrepreneurs for a higher value—an opportunity it quickly seized. Most of the people who had moved from the cities could not afford to pay the new market price and found themselves unemployed.[1] Peasants viewed the government's land policies as unjust, because they did nothing to help small farmers obtain land and they actively removed land from the hands of the citizens already in control of it.

From the 1930s onward, the government used its power to help wealthy landlords, making it easier for them to take over vast tracts of land and evict small farmers. As a result, a sense of injustice developed among Colombia's small farmers. Their resentment was directed at the Colombian government.

LA VIOLENCIA: 1948–1958

On April 9, 1948, Jorge Eliecer Gaitán, a prominent populist leader from the Liberal party, was assassinated in Bogotá. Gaitan's murder resulted in uprisings both of the Liberal Party supporters from the urban lower class and of the socialist-leaning poor. On that day, "La Violencia," a period characterized by violence and conflict between the Liberal and Conservative parties, began. During this time, self-defense groups started to emerge, acting under the name of the socialist sect of the Liberal Party. But the Liberal leadership, fearing that this violence would lead to a socialist rebellion, actively supporting repressive measures to eliminate the threat. In the early 1950s, Conservative president Laureano Gómez did just that, responding to the ongoing uprisings with violent repression.

In 1953 Gómez was overthrown by a military coup that brought General Gustavo Rojas Pinilla to power. Rojas Pinilla issued amnesty to all the armed peasants and responded to their call for agrarian reform by creating the Office of Rehabilitation and Relief. This office, however, did little to address the agrarian problem, failing to quell the peasant guerilla force in the countryside.[2] And once Rojas Pinilla resigned from office, the Conservative and Liberal elite implemented a power-sharing agreement called the National Front in an attempt to end the armed conflict. Starting in 1958, the two parties agreed to alternate four-year terms in the presidency. This agreement finally brought an end to the urban conflicts of "La Violencia." But the government still had to contend with the armed peasants.[3]

Part II: Creation of Guerillas and Paramilitary Groups

FARC (FUERZAS ARMADAS REVOLUCIONARIAS DE COLOMBIA)—1964

The oldest socialist peasant guerilla group in Colombia, the Revolutionary Armed Forces of Colombia (FARC), has its roots in the peasant struggles from the period of "La Violencia." Peasants from different parts of the countryside joined and met in the town of Marquetalia

1. Álvaro Albán, "Reforma y Contrareforma Agraria en Colombia," *Revista de Economía Institucional* 13, no. 24 (2011): 327–356, http://www.economiainstitucional.com/pdf/No24/aalban24.pdf.
2. Gary Leech, "Fifty Years of Violence," special report, *Colombia Journal* (May 1999), http://colombiajournal.org/fiftyyearsofviolence.
3. Ibid.

in 1961 to organize a larger peasant guerilla organization. In 1964 the government, led by President Guillermo Leon Valencia, launched an attack known as the "Operación Marquetalia" to target the socialist guerilla group—but the guerilla leadership learned about the attack before it occurred, and most of the members evacuated the area. When the military arrived, only 50 people were left. After that day, Manuel Marulanda, the leader of the group, officially founded the FARC.

At the beginning, the FARC was simply a rural guerilla force, but by the 1970s the group had expanded, becoming a true revolutionary army.[4] From the late 1980s through the beginning of the twenty-first century, the FARC reached its peak in both criminality and control over rural territory. The group became involved with drug trafficking to fund and expand their organization. The members began to receive military training and "colonized" territories where there was little or no state presence. During the same period, the FARC began to act as a terrorist force, murdering, kidnapping, and displacing thousands of people.[5]

The FARC's power diminished in the beginning of the twenty-first century, thanks to the implementation of Plan Colombia by President Andrés Pastrana. Under presidents Álvaro Uribe and Juan Manuel Santos, the FARC has weakened still more, as prominent FARC leaders have been killed, hostages have been rescued, and the FARC's territorial presence and armed activity has decreased. During this period especially, state presence increased in formerly FARC-controlled rural areas. At the time of writing this report, the FARC is engaged in the process of peace negotiations with the government.

ELN (EJÉRCITO DE LIBERACIÓN NACIONAL)—1965

Similar to the origins of the FARC, the National Liberation Army (ELN)'s roots also began with the rural conflicts from the period of "La Violencia." The ELN was formed in 1965 in northeastern Colombia by left-wing students, Catholics, and intellectuals who supported the peasants in their fight against the government. In its beginnings, the ELN was influenced by Marxist ideology, fighting for socioeconomic equality in the country. Like the FARC, the ELN was at first an ideologically driven group, only later becoming a violent guerilla movement perpetrating countless human rights violations and participating in large-scale drug trafficking.[6]

During the late 1990s the ELN reached the peak of its power. The twenty-first century, however, has seen their ranks decrease from 4,000 to 1,500 members, and the ELN is now significantly weaker than the FARC. Still, according to the Colombian government, the ELN maintains a major presence in regions of illicit cultivation, illegal mining, and oil extraction and remains actively involved in drug trafficking.[7]

---

4. "La Historia de las FARC," *Revista Semana*, November 19, 2012, http://www.semana.com/politica/articulo/la-historia-farc/268079-3.
5. UN Regional Information Center for Western Europe (UNRIC), "The Guerilla Groups in Colombia," accessed August 2, 2013, http://www.unric.org/en/colombia/27013-the-guerilla-groups-in-colombia.
6. Ibid.
7. Ibid.

PARAMILTARY GROUPS—1980; AUC (AUTODEFENSAS UNIDAS DE COLOMBIA)—1997

The paramilitary organizations in Colombia emerged in the early 1980s during the administration of President Julio Cesar Turbay, fashioning themselves as a conservative armed force to oppose socialist guerilla groups in the countryside. Their goal was to defend conservative rural communities from the socialist guerilla presence. Regardless of their original goals, the paramilitary soon became as violent as the FARC and the ELN. Supported by drug-trafficking organizations, the groups came to commit kidnappings, tortures, and massacres throughout the country.[8]

In 1997 most regional paramilitary groups joined together to form one larger paramilitary umbrella organization, the United Self-Defense Forces of Colombia (AUC), which is primarily present in northwestern Colombia. The organization aimed to consolidate the different paramilitary groups to fight the FARC and the ELN, defending conservative ideals. Their participation in drug trafficking provided funding for their military training and for weapons for their members. According to the Colombian government, the AUC numbered around 6,000 military personnel at its height.[9]

Under President Álvaro Uribe's government, the AUC began a process of disarmament in 2004. The process should be over, but some AUC members have refused to give up their arms and are still actively involved in criminal activities.[10]

Part III: Emergence of Drug-Trafficking Organizations and Drug Violence

During the second half of the twentieth century, Colombia went through a long period of powerful influence by drug traffickers that permeated almost every layer of society. The production of coca leaves and the illegal trade of cocaine to the United States brought the country into a period of violence and lawlessness. Two key factors explain why the country proved a viable environment for drug production and trafficking: first, Colombia's socioeconomic inequality in the rural sector; and second, weak government presence in rural areas.

For decades peasants felt that they were victims of the government's unjust agricultural policies. The rural sector in Colombia has always had greater levels of poverty than the urban areas. And in the 1970s, when drug cartels started to emerge, peasants realized that growing coca leaves would give them twice as much income as would producing any legal crop. Government crop prices were low, which kept small formers in poverty. Even typically exploitative cartels and guerillas paid peasants more than what the government

---

8. Edgar de Jesús Velásquez Rivera, "Historia del Paramilitarismo en Colombia," *Historia (Sao Paulo)* 26, no. 1 (2007): 134–153, http://www.redalyc.org/articulo.oa?id=221014794012.
9. UNRIC, "The Guerilla Groups in Colombia."
10. Ibid.

offered for legal crops. This incentivized peasants to start growing coca and, at first, even to welcome the presence of the illegal armed groups that drove this new economy.[11]

The second factor was the principal cause for the success of the drug business. The lack of state presence in rural areas opened the way for guerillas, paramilitary groups, and most importantly drug cartels to gain and maintain control of areas suitable for cultivating coca. As guerilla groups began their expansion during the 1980s and gained control of more rural territories, they realized the profits that could be derived from coca production, kicking off their participation. Enabled by the lack of military presence in these areas, the FARC and ELN used threats and other forms of coercion to force peasants to cultivate coca leaves.[12]

PABLO ESCOBAR AND THE INDUSTRIALIZATION OF COCA

Coca cultivation in Colombia has been a long-standing tradition, with its roots going back to indigenous tribes during the precolonial era. In all countries in the Andean region—Peru, Ecuador, Bolivia, and Colombia—coca plantations and coca-leaf production are commonplace. Why, then, did Colombia lead in cocaine trafficking? What made Colombia different?

Drug trafficking in Colombia differs from drug trafficking in other Andean countries thanks largely to the country's biggest drug lord, Pablo Escobar. Escobar industrialized the production of coca leaves and transformed drug trafficking into an organized business. Escobar's organization—the Cartel of Medellín—began as a small drug cartel. By joining marijuana smugglers, Escobar's group soon learned about the growing U.S. demand for cocaine. The Cartel of Medellín discovered an efficient way of exporting cocaine to the United States—through small planes, as was common with marijuana at the time. Once Escobar took control of the cartel, he expanded the Colombian drug trade—and the high demand from the United States generated spectacular profits to keep the business growing. Escobar could afford better planes and advanced technology for cocaine production—and he could bribe government officials. At his peak, Escobar oversaw more than 80 percent of the drug trade to the United States, transforming drug trafficking from a street crime to an organized transnational business.[13]

Escobar's Medellín Cartel ran an empire of cocaine production and drug trafficking. Any politician or journalist who threatened to expose their criminal activities or to pursue legal sanctions was kidnapped and killed. Escobar had more armed men protecting him and his business than the government had police presence in his region. By means of

11. Alex García Pulgarín, "Narcotrafico en Colombia: Un problema creado en otra parte, importado y asumido como propio," May 2010, http://aprendeenlinea.udea.edu.co/revistas/index.php/red/article/viewFile/8637/7971.

12. Jorge Orlando Melo, *Narcotrafico y Democracia: La Experiencia Colombiana*, Biblioteca Luis Angel Arango Digital, accessed August 4, 2013, http://www.banrepcultural.org/blaavirtual/educacion/melo/droga/gerrila.htm.

13. Jacob Stringer, "Pablo Escobar," *Colombia Reports*, January 8, 2013, http://colombiareports.com/pablo-escobar/.

threats and bribes, Escobar enjoyed control over police officials and officers. But in 1993 Escobar was killed in a police raid. With his death, the Cartel of Medellín weakened. Ever since, drug production and trafficking in Colombia have been principally dominated by guerillas and paramilitary groups.[14]

Drug trafficking and illicit cultivation have created major problems for the Colombian rural population and inhibited economic growth and prosperity. Despite current progress in anti-drug policies and improved security in the rural sector, the drug history has deeply harmed Colombia's population.

Part IV: Major Issues with Rural Conflict

DISPLACEMENT OF THE RURAL POPULATION

Colombia's long history of rural conflict has had a negative impact on the country's society. One of the main issues has been the displacement of millions of people from the rural areas to the cities. According to a report by the Colombian National Center of Historic Memory, more than 4.5 million Colombians have been displaced from rural areas by guerilla forces—primarily the FARC, paramilitary groups, and drug cartels.[15] These illegal armed groups take control of small farmers' land, forcing them either to join them and collaborate in coca cultivation, or to leave their land. Millions of unfairly displaced peasants migrate to the cities with no economic resources, no employment, and no shelter.[16]

HUMAN RIGHTS VIOLATIONS

Human rights violations in rural areas by guerillas, paramilitary groups, and drug cartels have impacted more of the Colombian population than any other aspect of the conflict. The Colombian National Center of Historic Memory reported that there were 27,000 confirmed kidnappings between 1970 and 2010. Of those cases, 24,000 were authored by FARC and ELN, and 3,000 by paramilitary groups. Hostages were generally subjected to brutal forms of torture during their time in captivity and were kept under inhumane conditions. In the past 30 years these illegal armed groups have also committed 150,000 murders.[17] Colombian society has been characterized by decades of human rights violations, particularly in the rural sector. And with no government presence in these areas, the rural population was left essentially on its own, with no protection against such abuses.

---

14. Ibid.

15. "Guerra en Colombia deja 220 mil muertos en 55 años: Centro de Memoria Histórica," RCN Radio, July 24, 2013, http://www.rcnradio.com/noticias/guerra-en-colombia-deja-220-mil-muertos-en-54-anos-revela-estudio-del-centro-de-memoria.

16. "La Hora de la Colombia Rural," *Hechos de Paz* 63 (2011): 2–16, http://www.pnud.org.co/hechosdepaz/echos/pdf/63.pdf.

17. "Una Sociedad Secuestrada," *Revista Semana*, June 22, 2013, http://www.semana.com/nacion/articulo/una-sociedad-secuestrada/348454-3.

COLOMBIAN POLITICAL AND ECONOMIC STABILITY IS THREATENED

The armed conflict in Colombia has harmed Colombia's economy. The lack of state presence, the power of drug-trafficking organizations and illegal armed groups, and the far-reaching violence in rural areas have prevented economic development in much of the country. Most of Colombia's useful natural resources and arable land for cultivation are found in the rural areas. With no government presence in these areas, guerillas and paramilitary groups took control of these lands and initiated violence.

This situation presented two problems: first, it inhibited investment as entrepreneurs and businesses refused to funnel their money toward high-risk locations; and second, a large quantity of arable land was wasted or used for illicit cultivation, rendering it useless to the legal economy.[18] Despite Colombia's vast resources, the armed conflict has prevented the country from prospering economically.

In a country dominated by violence, the governments throughout the past 30 years have prioritized security and defense policies over economic and development ones. The armed conflict has forced previous administrations to focus on policies that target drug trafficking and illegal armed groups. The violence throughout the country rendered these policies absolutely necessary. Until the start of the twenty-first century, this dynamic prevented the government from focusing on economic growth in the way that a country at peace would—though its efforts to maintain a growing economy have proven relatively successful, particularly in light of the challenges posed by the conflict.[19]

Part V: Plan Colombia

Table 1. Data on Plan Colombia

	Colombia	*United States*
Initial financial aid	US$4 billion	US$1.5 billion
Total financial aid	US$6.9 billion	US$3.7 billion
Casualties because of armed conflict	220,000	

Sources: U.S. embassy in Bogotá; *Semana* magazine; Council on Foreign Relations.

PRESIDENT ANDRÉS PASTRANA—1998–2002

In 2000 under President Andrés Pastrana, the Colombian and U.S. governments teamed up to begin Plan Colombia. This project aimed to improve the situation in rural areas and end the armed conflict by reducing drug trafficking, increasing economic development,

18. Salomon Kalmanovitz, "El impacto económico del conflicto interno," Programa de las Naciones Unidas para el Desarrollo (PNUD), http://pnud.org.co/img_upload/36353463616361636163616361636163/El_impacto_econ%C3%B3mico_del_conflicto_interno_colombiano_y_un_escenario_de_paz_Salom%C3%B3n_Kalmanovitz.pdf.

19. Francisco E. Thoumi, "Los efectos económicos de la industria de drogas ilegales y las agendas de política en Bolivia, Colombia y Perú," *Colombia Internacional* 29 (March 1995).

promoting peace talks, and ultimately improving security in rural Colombia. The Clinton administration joined Pastrana's efforts to improve Colombia's security and economy, starting with US$1.3 billion in aid and supporting the Colombian armed forces with military training and advanced military technology.[20]

Despite having introduced Plan Colombia, the Pastrana administration committed errors in the implementation of its security strategy. In 1998 Pastrana formed a zone free of armed forces to conduct peace talks in an attempt to secure the negotiations. This plan, known as "el despeje del Caguan," gave the territory in the region of Caguan—totaling 42,000 square kilometers—to the FARC.

This strategy proved disastrous, as the FARC took the land and continued committing criminal and terrorist activities. Because the government had removed its entire security presence from the region, the FARC quickly took control, violating the human rights of the area's people.[21] This situation was one of the greatest setbacks in the process for peace in Colombia—though with the implementation of Plan Colombia and the work of later presidents, the situation later improved.

PRESIDENT ÁLVARO URIBE—2002–2010

President Uribe continued to pursue Plan Colombia as part of his security platform once in office. Under his administration, and most noticeably because of his commitment to the policy's success, Plan Colombia made the most progress in terms of improving security in rural areas and increasing state presence in the countryside. In 2004 Uribe established government presence in all of Colombia's 1,099 municipalities—the first time that all of the country's regions enjoyed state presence.[22] With hopes of achieving peace, in 2005 the Uribe administration passed the Justice and Peace Law, which aimed to dismantle the AUC and disarm paramilitary soldiers by allowing them to provide information of their crimes in exchange for access to a transitional justice system. Even though the law was effective at reducing the size of the paramilitary forces, AUC factions joined or formed criminal gangs, or *Bandas Criminales* (BACRIM), focusing mainly on drug trafficking throughout the country.[23]

FALSOS POSITIVOS

Despite Uribe's success in improving security and furthering Plan Colombia, there were major scandals and controversies during his administration. Under Uribe, the government offered awards to soldiers for their accomplishments against guerillas, leading to the scandal known as the *Falsos Positivos* (False Positives).

---

20. U.S. Embassy in Bogotá, "Plan Colombia," accessed August 5, 2013, http://Bogotá.usembassy.gov/plancolombia.html.

21. "Consejo de Estado condenó a la Nación por despeje del Caguán," *El Espectador*, June 5, 2013, http://www.elespectador.com/noticias/judicial/articulo-426154-consejo-de-estado-condeno-nacion-despeje-del-caguan.

22. U.S. Embassy in Bogotá, "Plan Colombia."

23. Marcus Sales, "Plan Colombia years: A tainted success?" *Colombia Politics*, May 19, 2013, http://www.colombia-politics.com/plan-colombia-democracy/.

The False Positives scandal involved the killing of civilians and dressing them in guerilla uniforms by the Colombian military to increase body counts against guerilla forces—supposedly incentivized by Uribe's performance-based rewards. According to a report by the International Federation of Human Rights, between 2002 and 2008 there may have been over 3,000 False Positives killings.[24]

JUAN MANUEL SANTOS—2010–2014

After his election in 2010, President Juan Manuel Santos continued to pursue the goals of Plan Colombia. He furthered strategies to combat the armed guerillas and the paramilitary forces and joined in international efforts to stop drug trafficking, refocusing the security strategy to accelerate the structural weakening of the FARC, the ELN, and the criminal gangs (BACRIM). According to the U.S. Embassy in Colombia, Plan Colombia has, since its inception, helped reduce illicit cultivations by 40 percent, cocaine production by 60 percent, homicides by 50 percent, and terrorism and kidnappings by 90 percent.[25]

PEACE TALKS

One of President Santos's most important strategies to end violence in Colombia has been his peace negotiations process with the FARC. On November 19, 2012, the Santos government met with FARC leadership in Havana to commence peace negotiations.

The peace talks are set to include main issues such as: agrarian reform and development, political participation, drug trafficking, the rights of the victims of violence, and an end of armed conflict, and a system for the agreement's implementation.[26] So far, the issues of land reform and political participation have been resolved, with the two sides still in negotiations on the remaining four. The negotiations have been highly controversial; many prominent political figures in Colombia—such as former president Uribe—believe that the FARC does not deserve negotiations, given their status as a terrorist group whose members have violated the rights of millions of Colombian citizens. With the peace process, however, Santos remains optimistic, aiming to end 50 years of violence and to overcome the rural conflict.

Part VI: Current Situation with the Development of the Rural Sector

At the beginning of his time in office, President Juan Manuel Santos adopted a new agricultural policy and a new vision for rural growth and development in his National Development Plan—*Prosperidad Para Todos* (Prosperity for All). Santos's plan includes policies that aim to foster economic development, improve the formal distribution of land, bolster

24. Ibid.
25. U.S. Embassy in Bogotá, "Plan Colombia."
26. "Diez puntos claves del proceso," *Revista Semana*, October 18, 2012, http://www.semana.com/politica/articulo/diez-puntos-clave-del-proceso/266501-3.

transportation infrastructure, and ramp up security in rural areas by increasing governmental presence.[27]

Recently the government passed the Victims and Land Restitution Law (*Ley de Víctimas y Restitución de Tierras*), which aims to give property titles to populations that were previously displaced. With more than 4.5 million displaced people, this law looks to provide economic support to farmer families to grow crops and eventually create sustainable agricultural businesses.[28] Likewise, the government approved the Land and Rural Development Law project (*Ley de Tierras y Desarrollo Rural*), which aims to generate income for small farmers as well as to provide public services that can improve living conditions in rural areas. This act would legalize property rights and encourage wealthy landowners to develop their lands by modernizing technology and generating formal employment.[29]

27. "Plan de Desarrollo Nacional-Resumen Ejecutivo," Departamento Nacional de Planeacion, 2010.
28. "Ley Victimas y Restitucion de Tierras," Ministerio de Interior, 2011.
29. "Proyecto Ley de Tierras y Desarrollo Rural," Ministerio de Agricultura, 2012.

3 | Security
By Douglas Farah

Over the past 15 years Colombia has undergone a remarkable and profound positive transformation, particularly regarding its internal security. The stability, strength of its democratic institutions, and booming economy are proof of a decade of policies that have pulled Colombia back from the brink of collapse.

For the first time in its history, the state has a presence in each of the nation's 1,102 municipalities. Although pockets of the country remain under the influence of a variety of nonstate armed actors, by almost every measure today Colombia is a more safe and stable country. This is also a testament to the greatly increased professionalization and training of the Colombian police and military, and to the sustained bipartisan U.S. policy that spanned three presidencies and has led to a successful partnership that is unique in Latin America.

A few data points stand out. The land used for the cultivation of coca, the raw material for cocaine, has been cut in half, from a high of 99,000 hectares (251,400 acres) in 1999 to 48,000 hectares (122,000 acres).[1] Rather than producing 90 percent of the world's cocaine, Colombia now produces less than 60 percent.[2] Homicides per 100,000 inhabitants have dropped from 70.2 in 2002 to 30 in 2012. The most significant drops occurred in the cities of Bogotá and Medellín.[3]

As the conflict has moved into a different phase against more diffuse and less structured set of actors, U.S. aid has been steadily dropping. Although Colombia is still one of the top recipients of U.S. aid in the world, the downward trend—from $441.5 million in 2009 to $279.5 million in 2013 and a projected $257.6 million in 2014[4]—is likely irreversible.

Yet even at its peak during the Uribe administration—$611 million in 2004—U.S. aid never accounted for more than 26 percent of Colombia's national security budget. The rest

1. UN Office on Drugs and Crime (UNODC), "Colombia: Coca Cultivation Survey 2012," June 2013, http://www.unodc.org/documents/crop-monitoring/Colombia/Colombia_Coca_Cultivation_Survey_2012_web.pdf.
2. Data provided by the Colombian National Police and supported by U.S. government figures.
3. Edward Fox, "Colombia's Yearly Homicide Rate Sees 7% Drop," InSightCrime, December 7, 2012, http://www.insightcrime.org/news-briefs/colombia-yearly-homicide-rate-sees-7-drop.
4. "Just the Facts: A Civilian's Guide to U.S. Defense and Security Assistance to Latin America and the Caribbean," a joint project of Center for International Policy, Washington Office on Latin America, and the Latin America Working Group, http://justf.org/All_Grants_Country.

Map 1. Conflict and the Extractive Industries

Many of Colombia´s internal conflicts are driven by ilicit armed group´s acces to lucrative mining, petroleum, and natural gas sites, wich they use to finance themselves. They can do this by taxing and extorting companies that do the extraction, as is the case of the oil industry and some types of mining. This map shows the relationship between areas of extraction and violence.

1 Petroleum and gas: Areas in extraction

2 Legal Mining Titles

3 Municipalities that experienced at least one incident related to the armed conflict in 2012

4 Municipalities that did not experience any event related to the armed conflict in 2012

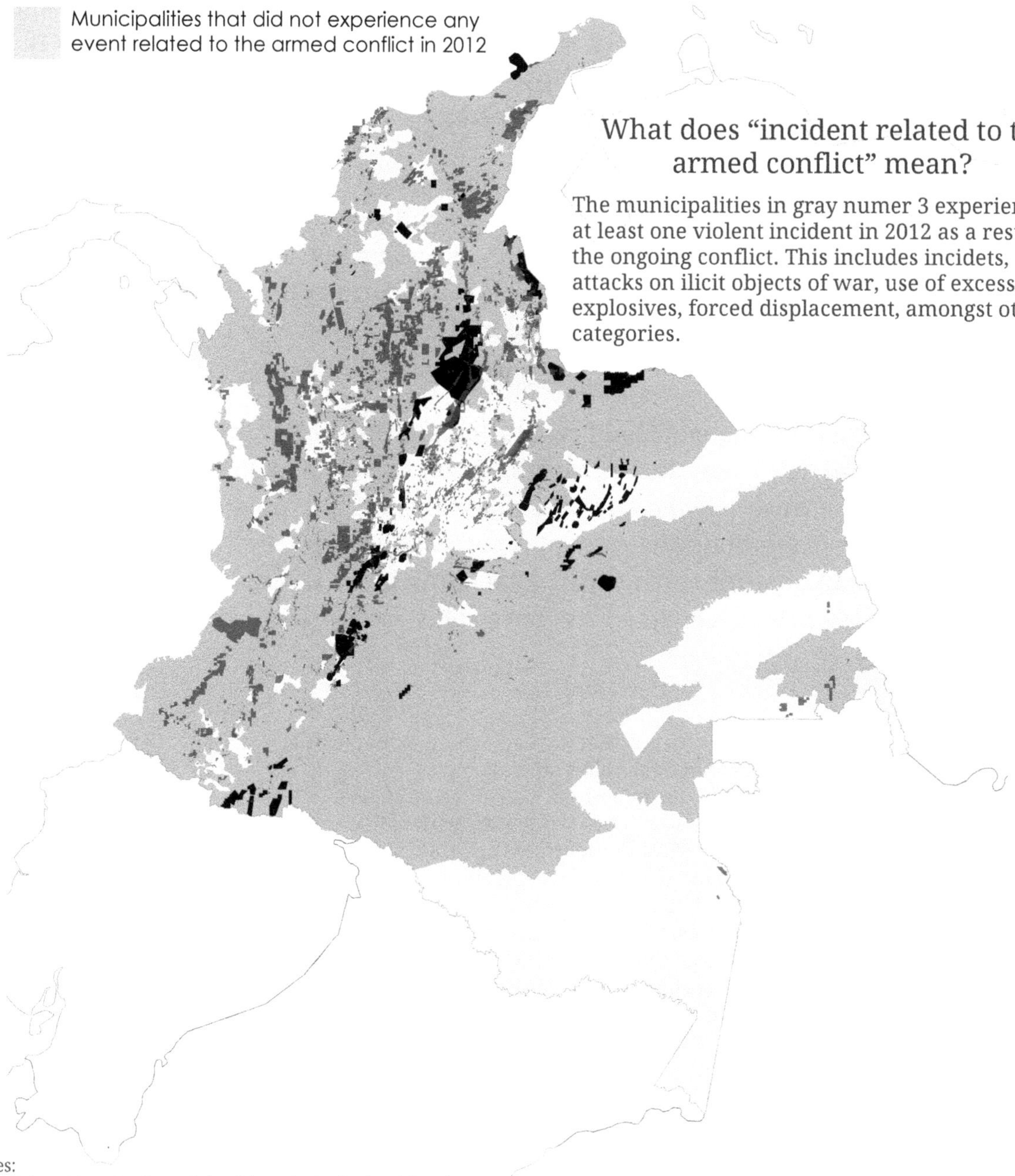

What does "incident related to the armed conflict" mean?

The municipalities in gray numer 3 experienced at least one violent incident in 2012 as a result of the ongoing conflict. This includes incidets, attacks on ilicit objects of war, use of excess war explosives, forced displacement, amongst other categories.

Sources:
Legal mining titles: *Instituto Colombiano de Geología y Minería*, 2012.
Hydrocarbon areas in extraction: *Agencia Nacional de Hidrocarburos*, 2013.
Incidents of the armed conflict: UN OCHA Colombia, SIDIH, 2012.

has come from Colombian resources generated by higher taxes, mostly levied on businesses and the wealthy, to pay for the Colombian part of the budget.[5] The percentage of U.S. support had dropped to 4 percent by 2012 and is projected to be 3 percent in 2014, while the overall defense budget continues to increase slightly through the same period.[6]

Yet in a country that has been in an almost continual state of internal conflict for more than 50 years and where undisputed state authority has been absent for centuries, the gains remain fragile and reversible. Government officials recognize that citizen security and a positive state presence are essential to any path toward durable peace and economic growth.[7]

Colombia's internal violence is complex and historic, defying easy analysis or solutions. Even as the state security apparatus becomes more efficient, more effective, and more respectful of human rights, the drivers of insecurity, as they have over the past five decades, continue to mutate into new and lethal forms.

FARC is badly weakened, but other armed actors are shifting the internal conflict to pockets of natural resource extraction, where powerful groups have entrenched interests and a strong, armed presence. As the UN High Commission for Refugees noted in its 2013 country report, "the effects on the environment of gold mining and the extraction of other natural resources, compounded by the influence of armed groups in these activities, has had a devastating impact on civilians."[8]

Particularly in issues related to land restitution, the emerging "criminal gangs," *Bandas Criminales* (BACRIM), are a new and disturbing factor in murders, kidnappings, and the intimidation of those who seek to claim land under the Victims and Land Restitution Law of 2011.[9] In 2011 the Colombian government reported there were five BACRIM structures operating in 118 municipalities out of 1,102 total municipalities. Currently most of those BACRIM groups have been decapitated and have splintered into smaller groups operating on a regional level.

---

5. Author interviews with U.S. and Colombian officials.
6. Data provided to the author by the Colombian Ministry of Defense.
7. The concept of "positive state presence" draws on the work of Robert H. Jackson, *Quasi-States: Sovereignty, International Relations and the Third World* (New York: Cambridge University Press, 1990). Jackson defines negative sovereignty as freedom from outside interference, the ability of a sovereign state to act independently, both in its external relations and internally, toward its people. Positive sovereignty is the acquisition and enjoyment of capacities, not merely immunities. In Jackson's definition, it presupposes "capabilities which enable governments to be their own masters" (29). The absence of either type of sovereignty can lead to the collapse or absence of state control. See also Anne L. Clunan and Harold A. Trinkunas, "Conceptualizing Ungoverned Spaces," in *Ungoverned Spaces: Alternatives to State Authority in an Era of Softened Sovereignty*, ed. Anne L. Clunan and Harold A. Trinkunas (Stanford, CA: Stanford University Press, 2010).
8. UN High Commissioner for Refugees (UNHCR), "Colombia: 2013 UNHCR country operations profile," http://www.unhcr.org/pages/49e492ad6.html.
9. Human Rights Watch, *The Risk of Returning Home: Violence and Threats against Displaced People Reclaiming Land in Colombia* (New York: Human Rights Watch, September 2013), http://www.hrw.org/sites/default/files/reports/colombia0913webwcover.pdf.

THE HARD-WON PATH TOWARD A SAFER STATE

Colombia is now viewed as one of the most dynamic nations in the hemisphere. Nevertheless, enormous challenges remain in consolidating the gains made and combatting the new types of violence over natural resources, commodities, and illicit trafficking routes.

In the late 1990s Colombia was one of the most violent nations in the world, despite having eliminated the infamous Medellín and Cali cartels. The FARC, right-wing paramilitary "self-defense" groups, and drug-trafficking organizations controlled more than half the national territory. Colombia was the world's largest producer of cocaine, as well as coca leaves, the raw material for cocaine.

The situation sank to its lowest point in the late 1990s when President Ernesto Samper's U.S. visa publicly revoked for Samper's alleged ties to the Cali cartel. The chairman of the Colombian military's Joint Chiefs of Staff met the same fate, and the military was in complete disarray.

At the same time the army suffered a string of humiliating defeats at the hands of the FARC, which was evolving into a significant drug-trafficking organization.

A 1998 assessment by the U.S. Defense Intelligence Agency (DIA) found that the FARC and its allies in drug trafficking would be able to defeat the government within five years, converting Colombia into a "narco-state." The commander of the U.S. Southern Command at the time testified in Congress, "The primary vulnerability of the Colombian armed forces is their inability to see threats, followed closely by their lack of competence in assessing and engaging them."[10]

When President Andrés Pastrana agreed in 1999 to peace talks with the FARC and granted them a territory the size of Switzerland as a demilitarized zone, the Colombian government was at its weakest point. In addition to the military defeats, the economy was sinking. Poverty rates had risen dramatically, unemployment was growing, and the economy sank by more than 4 percent in 1999.

The FARC, with some 20,000 combatants and flush with sophisticated new weapons and equipment purchased with money from its burgeoning drug trade, was at its strongest point militarily since it was founded in 1964.

During the three-year negotiations, which ended in February 2002, the FARC significantly strengthened itself and its ties to cocaine trafficking while dragging the talks on with endless and constantly shifting demands. But the military, given a reprieve, also used the time to reorganize, train, and dramatically improve it capabilities.[11]

---

10. Douglas Farah, "Colombian Rebels Seen Winning War; U.S. Study Finds Army Inept, Ill-Equipped," *Washington Post*, April 10, 1998, http://colombiasupport.net/archive/199804/wp41098.html.

11. For an excellent overview of this process, see previous CSIS reports on Colombia, particularly Peter DeShazo, Tanya Primiani, and Phillip McLean, *Back from the Brink: Evaluating Progress in Colombia, 1999–2007*

With the election of Álvaro Uribe in 2002, Colombia's military turnaround began in earnest. Under Uribe's program of "Democratic Security," raw recruits were replaced over time with a highly trained NCO corps; intelligence operations were revamped and enhanced, and significant new Colombia resources were committed to the conflict.

Uribe also underscored the important link between democracy and security, stating consistently that the overarching goal was to "reinforce and guarantee the rule of law in all our national territory." As the government raised taxes and showed results, the businesses and citizens in urban areas became more supportive of the government.

Although Uribe would come under significant and justified criticism from human rights groups for illicitly spying on journalists and political enemies and tolerating human rights abuses in the military,[12] he is widely credited with developing the first comprehensive plan—including programs encompassing judicial, infrastructure rehabilitation, education, and medical programs to reestablish government authority in areas where nonstate actors had held sway for generations.

Focusing on rapidly accelerating military operations against the FARC and the group's drug-trafficking infrastructure, Uribe and his military leadership designed a strategy that pushed the guerrillas out of the economically vital middle section of the country and away from cities and important transportation routes. It also aimed to do away with their leadership.

Part of the urgency of confronting the FARC was the fact that presidents Hugo Chávez of Venezuela and Rafael Correa of Ecuador were giving significant logistical, financial, and political support to the FARC, allowing FARC to expand its international networks. Captured FARC documents revealed that Correa's 2006 presidential campaign had received significant donations from the FARC.[13]

On March 1, 2008, the Colombian military launched an assault that would dramatically alter the course of the conflict. The attack on the military headquarters of Raúl Reyes, the FARC second-in-command, located in Ecuador, killed Reyes and captured several hundred gigabytes of data the FARC commander had stashed at the camp.

While setting off a diplomatic row, the attack also accomplished two significant things: it captured years' worth of internal FARC communications that greatly enhanced the operational understanding of the group, and it killed a senior FARC commander, the first member of the guerrillas' general secretariat to be killed in combat in 44 years of war. Reyes's death was followed by the killing of other high-value FARC targets, as well as a

(Washington, DC: CSIS, November 2007), http://csis.org/files/media/csis/pubs/071112-backfromthebrink-web.pdf.

12. For a comprehensive look at the positive and negative aspects of the Uribe government, see June S. Beittel, "Colombia: Background, U.S. Relations, and Congressional Interest," Congressional Research Service, November 28, 2012, http://www.fas.org/sgp/crs/row/RL32250.pdf.

13. For a look at documented financial and logistical support of Chávez and Correa for the FARC, based on captured FARC documents, see "The FARC Files: Venezuela, Ecuador and the Secret Archives of 'Raúl Reyes,'" IISS Strategic Dossier, International Institute for Strategic Studies, May 2011.

stream of desertions of many mid-level and upper-level commanders, sending the FARC into a downward military and financial spiral from which has never recovered.[14]

While focusing on a military solution with the FARC, the Uribe government also engaged in a controversial disarmament and demobilization program with the paramilitary groups who were also deeply involved in drug trafficking and had committed an enormous amount of human rights violations, including countless massacres, forced disappearances, kidnappings, and other crimes.

The program drew significant criticism[15] but did succeed, at least on paper, in demobilizing more than 30,000 members of the United Self-Defense Forces of Colombia (*Autodefensas Unidas de Colombia*—AUC), most of whose leaders were extradited to the United States.

However, several thousand of the demobilized AUC members have formed their own BACRIM or joined existing criminal groups, remaining a significant factor in the violence that continues, particularly in drug trafficking and land seizures.[16] In some cases, particularly in Putumayo along the Ecuadoran border, former AUC combatants now collaborate with the FARC in drug trafficking and illicit mining ventures.

TODAY'S SECURITY CHALLENGES

The constant ability of nonstate armed actors to morph into new types of groups deriving income from different sources to fund their activities is perhaps the greatest security challenge facing Colombia today.

This is particularly difficult because the state security forces are having to simultaneously assume the costly and resource-intensive task of holding significant parts of the country where the central government is seeking to reestablish its authority while continuing to clear new areas of the different armed groups largely operating in rugged jungle terrain.

The security forces have been remarkably successful in significantly reducing the existential threats to the state (major cartels, the FARC, and the AUC). But they are now facing a more dispersed series of actors that continue to undermine state sovereignty and diminish the state's ability to regain the trust of its citizens and establish the rule of law.

---

14. For a more complete look at the role of Ecuador and the FARC, see Douglas Farah and Glenn Simpson, *Ecuador at Risk: Drugs, Thugs, Guerrillas and the Citizens Revolution* (Alexandria, VA: International Assessment and Strategy Center, January 2010), http://www.strategycenter.net/docLib/20101214_EcuadorFINAL.pdf. For a study of Venezuela's role with the FARC, see Douglas Farah *Transnational Organized Crime, Terrorism, and Criminalized States in Latin America: An Emerging Tier-One National Security Priority* (Carlisle, PA: Strategic Studies Institute, August 2012), http://www.strategicstudiesinstitute.army.mil/pubs/display.cfm?pubID=1117.

15. See, for example, Human Rights Watch, *Smoke and Mirrors: Colombia's Demobilization of Paramilitary Groups* (New York: Human Rights Watch, August 2005), http://www.hrw.org/reports/2005/colombia0805/colombia0805.pdf.

16. For a more comprehensive look at the history of the AUC, the problems with its demobilization, and the extraditions of its top leadership, see International Human Rights Law Clinic, *Truth behind Bars: Colombian Paramilitary Leaders in U.S. Custody* (Berkeley, CA: International Human Rights Law Clinic, February 2010), http://www.law.berkeley.edu/files/IHRLC/Truthbehindbars.pdf.

Even though the FARC has been reduced from its peak of more than 20,000 combatants to about 7,000 today, they pose a significant local threat in areas where they operate, generally relying on small-unit ambushes and constant movement to avoid large-scale combat. Another Marxist guerrilla group. the National Liberation Army (*Ejército de Liberación Nacional*—ELN), also involved in drug trafficking, has some 1,500 combatants, and the BACRIM groups number some 3,700 armed members. Across the country there are several thousand more armed criminal gangs are operating on a smaller scale, and with less military coherence, in a more localized manner.

Reestablishing a state presence is particularly difficult in areas where the state has seldom had a presence at all, and where nonstate groups have exercised sovereignty. In these areas the "culture of illegality" has thrived for generations, where the state is viewed as the illicit interloper and local political structure has virtually no ties to or response from the central government. In many cases, earlier human rights abuses of the military have left the local population hostile and wary of a renewed state presence.

One example of the new challenges that emerge even as traditional ones subside is the illicit trade in coltan and gold, both valuable minerals whose exploitation carries far less risk than the cocaine trade. Yet the illicit mining spawns armed groups, drives civilians from their land, causes significant ecological damage, and is a constant local driver of violence. The FARC, along with multiple other criminal groups, often with ties to drug-trafficking organizations, are increasingly involved in illicit mineral extraction.[17]

These new challenges mean that the security forces must be highly adaptable and reconfigured to meet more diverse challenges at a time when both U.S. and national resources are likely to diminish. It also means that the nation's security forces will have to learn to coordinate extremely closely with a host of civilian agencies and often cede the lead role to the civilians. This clash of cultures continues to pose significant challenges among different agencies involved in the consolidation process.

In recognition of these new challenges the Santos government in 2012 launched Campaign Sword of Honor (*Espada de Honor*), with the goal of launching a simultaneous offensive in the remaining base areas of FARC and ELN in order to deliver a decisive strategic defeat and combat the BACRIM and its illicit networks.

The operation, including the formation of 12 new regional joint task forces and intelligence fusion centers, focuses on 15 of the FARC's 67 combat fronts that are most active and most involved in the cocaine trade, and aims to reduce the FARC's size by 50 percent over two years. The campaign focuses on the most critical fronts in terms of command and control, terrorist activity, and financing, aiming at bringing FARC to half of its structural capabilities.[18]

---

17. For an extensive report on the illicit coltan trade, see Ignacio Gómez, "Colombia's Black-Market Coltan Tied to Drug Trafficking, Paramilitaries," Center for Public Integrity, March 4, 2012, http://www.publicintegrity.org/2012/03/04/8284/colombia-s-black-market-coltan-tied-drug-traffickers-paramilitaries.
18. For a more in-depth look at Operation Sword of Honor, see Colby Martin, "Colombia's New

In order to be able to bring legal charges—rather than lethal force—against the networks of civilian supports for the FARC and other violent groups, the task forces include judicial police and government prosecutors.[19] After initially starting in 51 municipalities, the operation has now grown to include 58 townships in the most vulnerable regions of the country.[20]

Reflecting the changing nature of the conflict, the military high command has concluded that 52 of the 67 FARC fronts are no longer under the direct command and control of the general secretariat and are turning increasingly to criminal activities based on whatever resources are available to them in their areas of operation.[21]

The FARC's growing lack of command-and-control capabilities over most of its fronts has significant implications for both the future FARC and the government's efforts to defeat it on the battlefield. There is a strong possibility, already seen in some areas of FARC operation, that the group's combat fronts will simply drift off into criminal activity, while perhaps keeping some sort of loose allegiance to and alliance with the FARC high command.[22]

This is but one of multiple difficulties remaining in the area of national security. Given the complexity of the internal conflicts and the geographically diverse regions that they span, addressing them within a single security policy is not an easy task.

CHALLENGES GOING FORWARD

A failure to adequately address the challenges mentioned could risk many of the hard-won gains achieved by the Colombian security forces in recent years. To their credit, leaders of the security forces are highly aware of the changing nature of the internal conflict and the need to revise and revisit many past assumptions and operational strategies and tactics that, though successful in the past, may not be adequate in the coming years.

The change from a force primarily focused on combating a structured insurgency with a centralized command and its overlapping cocaine-trafficking structures to a small-unit war with a wide variety of enemies is difficult on its own.

One of the biggest concerns of Colombian defense officials is the sustainability of the current policy at a time of declining U.S. aid and a growing weariness in the Colombian population over the level of taxation needed to sustain the effort. Not only do current levels

---

Counterinsurgency Plan," Stratfor, March 29, 2012, http://www.openbriefing.org/issuedesks/politicalviolence/espadadehonor/.

19. Information provided to the author by the Colombian Ministry of Defense.

20. Colombian vice minister of defense Jorge Bedoya, CSIS conference in Bogotá, Colombia, June 17, 2013.

21. Redacción Judicial, "Operación Espada de Honor: Rumbo que van a seguir las autoridades para enfrentar la amenaza de la guerrilla," *El Espectador*, February 18, 2012, http://www.elespectador.com/impreso/temadeldia/articulo-327286-operacion-espada-de-honor.

22. For a look at different scenarios for the FARC's evolution during the current peace process, see Jeremy McDermott, "Possible Scenarios for the FARC's Fragmentation," InSightCrime, May 20, 2013, http://www.insightcrime.org/farc-peace/scenarios-farc-fragmentation.

need to be sustained, but many will have to significantly expanded as the state pushes to establish a presence farther and farther afield.

There are also significant logistical costs and hardships associated with creating sufficient security in remote areas to enable the functioning of other state institutions, such as the judiciary, law enforcement, and road building, in those places. Compounding the problem is the need to hold territory where the civilian population for decades has either been overtly hostile to the state and sympathetic to nonstate actors, or has often been the victim of significant human rights abuses by the state.

Both factors make Herculean tasks of efforts to establish a positive state presence and a relatively secure environment and to sustaining the effort until the state presence can take root. Yet failure to meet any of these challenges could give nonstate armed actors enough space to prosper while failing to meet the expectations of an already-skeptical civilian population. Such disillusionment could lead to further support for nonstate actors, reigniting the cycle of violence.

Over the past decade Colombia has demonstrated the resolve to take many significant strides toward transforming the nation and eradicating the violence that has plagued it for generations. Many more strides remain to be taken.

Tolima
By Douglas Farah

Chaparral, Tolima—Few places in Colombia offer a more difficult test of the Colombian government's strategy of territorial consolidation than this dusty, sprawling township in south-central Tolima Province.

For more than four decades it was in the heart of a FARC stronghold, just a few miles north from where the guerrilla group was formed in 1964. The FARC's 21st Front carved out a command-and-control center here that was among the most important of the insurgency. Although only 150 miles south of Bogotá, the town was separated from the national capital by a steep mountain range and centuries of history.

Just how ensconced the FARC has remained in the region was shown by the fact that Alfonso Cano, the FARC's secretary general, sought sanctuary in outlying hideaways for several years while being pursued by the military. He was killed in a bombing raid in November 2011, shortly after moving his camp to neighboring Cauca Province.[23] Land mines planted by the FARC to protect its camps remain a serious problem for both the military and civilians in the region.

23. Cano's real name was Guillermo Leon Saenz, and he was a former academic turned guerrilla commander. The Colombian government called his death the "single biggest blow" against the FARC in the history of the war. See "Obituary: Alfonso Cano," BBC News, November 5, 2011, http://www.bbc.co.uk/news/world-latin-america-15604609.

Over the past 50 years political violence between the Liberal and Conservative parties, then the presence of the FARC, served to isolate Chaparral and its environs, with virtually no state presence or services. In turn its inhabitants have historically had little sense of allegiance to the national government.

Leonardo Avilés García, the head of Justice House (*Casa de Justicia*) program, partly funded by USAID and aimed at broadening the access of citizens to the judicial system, wept and softly sang an a cappella version of a ballad of how his family was killed and his village burned during the violence. "We lost 50 years to violence, the whole southern part of Tolima Province," he said. "Violence afflicted us all."

In recent decades the FARC were a much more tangible presence here than the government and, over time, set up rudimentary judicial and taxation systems while content to let the roads and other infrastructure wither in order to make it harder for the military to come into the area. The region was sympathetic to the insurgents from the birth of the movement, in part because many of the peasants could not buy land in a region controlled by large cattle ranchers and coffee growers.

Jaime Ospina, a local congressman and former mayor of Chaparral, said that when he was mayor, in 1982–1987, the FARC summoned him and other candidates for local office to their main camp to remind them that the FARC was the real power in the region and would be dictating the parameters of acceptable political activity. Over one six-year period the town had 12 mayors, as the FARC forced one after the other to resign under threat of death.

"They told us they were the state, and we would have to listen to them," Ospina said. "The FARC influenced everything. They would go into towns and call town meetings to indoctrinate and also demand an accounting from each town. Now it is a complete change."

Over the years the region proved a fertile recruiting ground for the FARC. Over the decades, many of the young people joined the armed movement or the local militias, which provided them food, logistical support, and intelligence. Their families provided a natural political base for the insurgents, and the FARC militias remain active in gathering intelligence and political work.

"There is not a family here who does not have a family member in the FARC," Ospina said. "It is a multigenerational phenomenon, 50 years in the making, and a source of great tension still."

Now the government teams working on "territorial consolidation" are undertaking the enormous task of trying to prove that the state—almost entirely absent from this town since the 1950s—can offer what the FARC or other nonstate armed groups that once occupied the territory could not: economic opportunity, infrastructure,

Map 2. Tolima

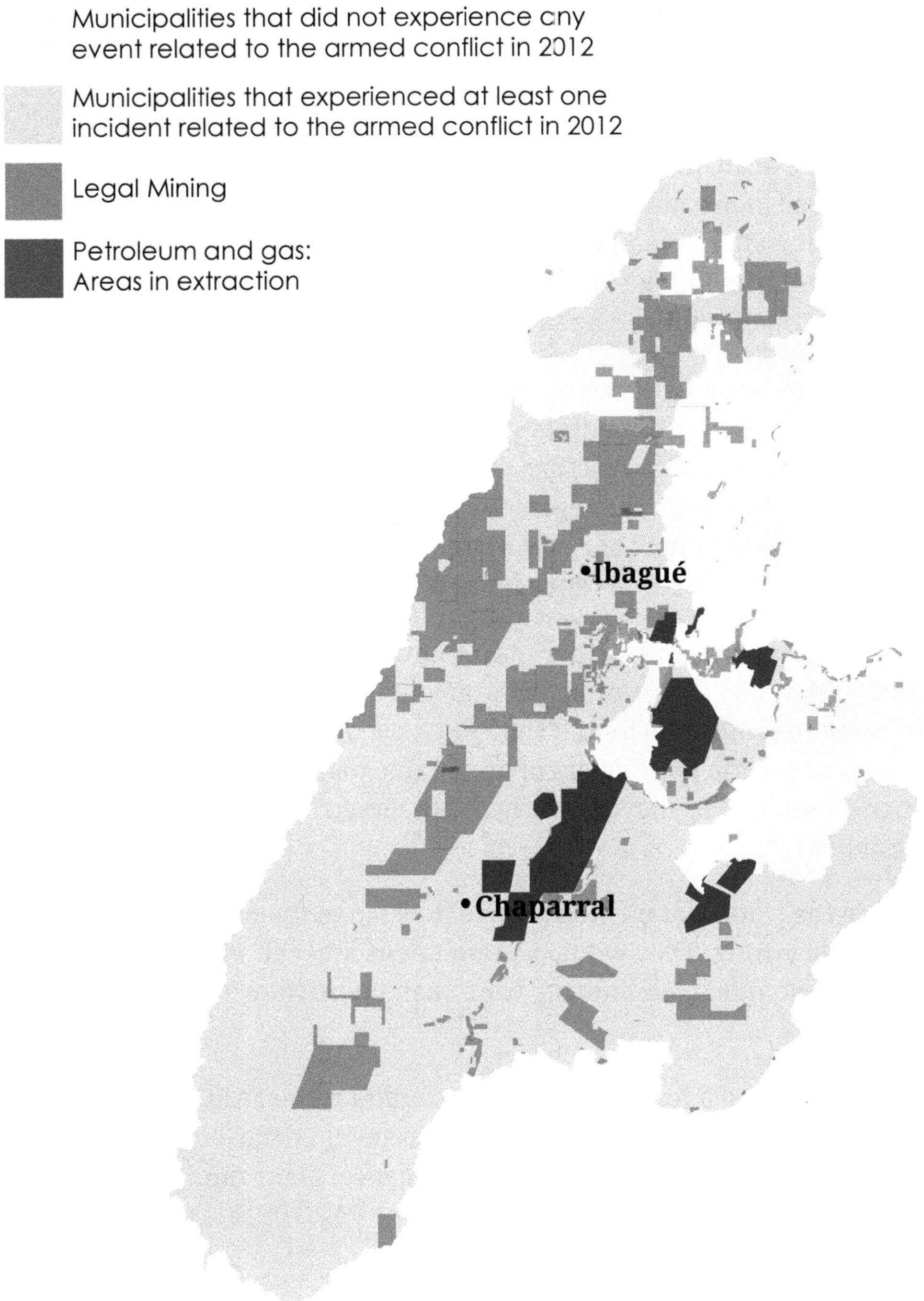

Sources:
Legal mining titles: *Instituto Colombiano de Geología y Minería, 2012.*
Hydrocarbon areas in extraction: *Agencia Nacional de Hidrocarburos, 2013.*
Incidents of the armed conflict: UN OCHA Colombia, SIDIH, 2012.

education; a judicial system, and legal title to land on which the people have lived for many years.

By all accounts Chaparral, a town of some 40,000, including the outlying hamlets, is has been transformed since being integrated into the government's consolidation program. Buses and private transport link the town to Ibagué, the departmental capital, 100 miles to the northeast, and Bogotá. Municipal officials such as the mayor and city council members live here, not in Ibagué, something that was unthinkable five years ago.

The town now has four functioning banks and a hotel, and stores are well stocked. Enough of the region's famed coffee is being harvested again to begin exporting some to the rest of Colombia, hopefully showing over time that private investment as well as public projects can return to the region.

A joint task force of military and police has successfully pushed the FARC far from the town and surrounding hamlets. The last skirmish with the guerrillas in the vicinity was in 2012. Signs of the expanding reach of the government are the official vehicles that crisscross the rutted dirt roads to inspect roadwork by the Army Corps of Engineers and other infrastructure projects. Slowly the state is extending the badly neglected network of secondary and tertiary roads that are necessary for commerce and transportation.

"The roads are the most important thing economically, and the issue of land titling is the biggest bottleneck we have to progress," said Chaparral mayor Hugo Arce. "Things are better, but change is very slow. We are trying to change Chaparral from a small town to a city. That is the radical change we are trying to bring about."

There are other positive indicators. The number of homicides in the township dropped from 63 in 2002 to 6 in 2012. Other indicators of violence, such as robberies and attacks, have also dropped significantly. Kidnappings, largely carried out by the FARC, are now a thing of the past.

Since Chaparral was declared part of the Consolidation program in 2008, residents and official say the biggest obstacle encountered so far has been building credible systems of land titling and land dispute adjudication.

Thousands of people have filed claim under the land restitution act, but often the land in question has been bought and sold numerous times with no records having been kept. There is really no baseline from which to start. According to local and national government officials, the process has been greatly hampered by the inability of judges to visit the sites of land disputes due to a lack of vehicles, money for fuel, and physical security.

"You have to understand, they stopped keeping land records here in the 1950s, with the violence of the time, and then the FARC presence," said Gustavo Rivet, one of two land judges, in Ibuagué. "If you ask someone how much land they have, they might say 20 hectares, but when you measure it, it is only thee hectares. Or they might say they have two hectares and it is 10. It is absolute chaos. We have eight land judges now, but it is not enough. It is not something we can move quickly to resolve, and we lack resources. But we know we have work fast or the process will lose credibility."

In an effort to jump-start the restitution process, the Santos government in September 2012 initiated the first process to take land belonging to the FARC in the town of Ataco, just south of here. The restitution claim was filed on behalf of 33 families claiming 200 hectares (508 acres) that the FARC had taken from the land's original owners. Because of the FARC's strong ties in the region, it was a symbolic move, the first of what the government said would be restitution claims for 700,000 hectares (1.8 million acres) taken by the FARC.[24]

At the headquarters of Joint Task Force Zeus, Major General Luis Eduardo Vargas said his ability to establish a permanent police presence in some of the hamlets was hampered by the fact that the land on which to build the police stations was in dispute. The police could not build unless the property was legally acquired, and it could not be purchased until the ownership claims were resolved.

Vargas, who commands the task force, said his forces have targeted the FARC's financial infrastructure in the region and have so reduced the remnants of the 21st Front that they must resort to kidnapping and extortion to fund their activities.

The Front currently has about 105 armed members, he said, less than half the number from two years ago. With two helicopters to keep his forces mobile and a joint military-police intelligence fusion unit operational, the FARC is a diminished presence. Intercepted communications show that the FARC's general secretariat has chastised the Front for its meager economic support for the high command and loss of territory, Vargas said.

"They can't take over towns, they can't do armed roadblocks or carry out kidnappings on a large scale," Vargas said. "They can move 10 to 12 people at a time, but now the population tells us where they are, so they are constantly mobile and on the run."

Militia structures still exist to aid the FARC in the region, but these are being neutralized through a combination of intelligence, shifting community loyalties, and

24. Daniel Valero, "Victimas relcaman 70,000 hectáreas robadas por la FARC: Primeras demandas para recuperar esas tierras se radican el miércoles en Tolima," *El Tiempo* (Bogotá), September 30, 2012, http://www.eltiempo.com/politica/victimas-reclaman-700000-hectareas-robadas-por-farc_12269101-4.

the use of police and judges to arrest and hold suspects, rather than treating them as armed combatants.

Residents complain that petty crimes like household robberies are increasing. Young people are increasingly smoking marijuana, and cattle rustling is on the rise. All of this is a challenge, but not of the magnitude of combating the FARC on a daily basis on hostile terrain.

Each success seems to bring another series of major challenges, residents here say, and managing expectations is difficult. Many complain that social investment is not coming fast enough, road building is not fast enough, and there is still a significant lack of coordination among the municipal governments, the provincial government, and the central government. Land titles are not being issued and resources are constantly scarce.

"The lack of credibility of the government is the Achilles' heel of the process," Ospina said. "The judicial work is not advancing as fast as other parts. There are few businesses generating employment. We grow the best coffee in Colombia but can't always get it to market. But we have advanced a lot. There is more of an institutional presence, the military is not committing as many human rights abuses, and the process of rescuing this region has begun."

Vargas said the need to keep the task force in place would be re-evaluated next year, to see if the resources of his group could be better utilized elsewhere as new towns and regions enter the Consolidation program, although there are no clear criteria for such an evaluation. And it is precisely that kind of talk that spooks local residents.

"We are at a crucial moment," Avilés Garcia said. "The FARC is not visibly present, but if the military isn't here they will come back and we will all lose. What good is it to recuperate territory if we can't stay to govern it afterward? Things are at a very delicate point. If they leave too soon, we could lose everything."

4 Land Tenure

By Douglas Farah

No issue lies at the heart of so many of Colombia's vexing and complex social problems and causes of violence as the issue of land tenure and ownership. And few issues are more difficult to resolve because of historic factors, vested interests, and the sheer scale of the challenge.

Although the Santos government has taken some historic steps to begin a long and costly process of setting up an orderly system for land reform and restitution of land to victims of the nation's internal violence, any significant progress will require enormous resources, political will, and perhaps decades to complete.

The cumulative effects of decades of conflict, often centered on land issues, have left a devastating legacy, driving nearly 5 million from their homes, creating the world's largest population of internally displaced persons (IDPs) in the world. Recent studies estimate that the IDPs' abandoned land, when taken together, would be roughly the size of Maryland and Massachusetts combined. Most of the land has been seized by armed groups or their allies, driving most of the destitute original owners to the nearest urban center, setting off a cascade of crises.[1]

In a 2010 assessment the U.S. Agency for International Development (USAID) concluded that in Colombia, "formalization of land rights is viewed not only as a mechanism to enhance tenure security and promote production but also a critical tool in efforts to prevent the spread of the humanitarian crisis surrounding displaced persons."[2]

The historic extreme inequality of arable land tenure and the subsequent rural unrest gave rise to most of the guerrilla groups that have emerged through the years, including the FARC and ELN, which are still fighting the government. Leaders of the Medellín cartel took over enough land in the Magdalena Medio region of Colombia in the mid-1980s to form a semi-independent republic. And the fearsome paramilitary groups committed uncounted

1. Human Rights Watch, *The Risk of Returning Home*. For additional information on this subject, see U.S. Department of State, *Country Reports on Human Rights Practices for 2012: Colombia*, 2012, http://www.state.gov/j/drl/rls/hrrpt/humanrightsreport/index.htm#wrapper; and UNHCR, "Colombia: 2013 UNHCR Country Operations Profile." http://www.unhcr.org/cgi-bin/texis/vtx/page?page=49e492ad6.

2. U.S. Agency for International Development (USAID), "USAID Program Brief: Land Tenure and Property Rights, Colombia," January 2010, http://usaidlandtenure.net/sites/default/files/USAID_Land_Tenure_Colombia_Program_Brief_0.pdf.

Map 3. Rural Land Distribution in Colombia

This map shows the Gini rural land index, demonstrating the concentration of quality, cultivable and in the hands of few owners. The Gini index measures distribution on a scale from 0 to 1. The closer the number is to 1, the more concentrated the land is (few owners, lots of land), whereas the closer the number is to 0, the more distributed it is (lots of owners, lots of land).

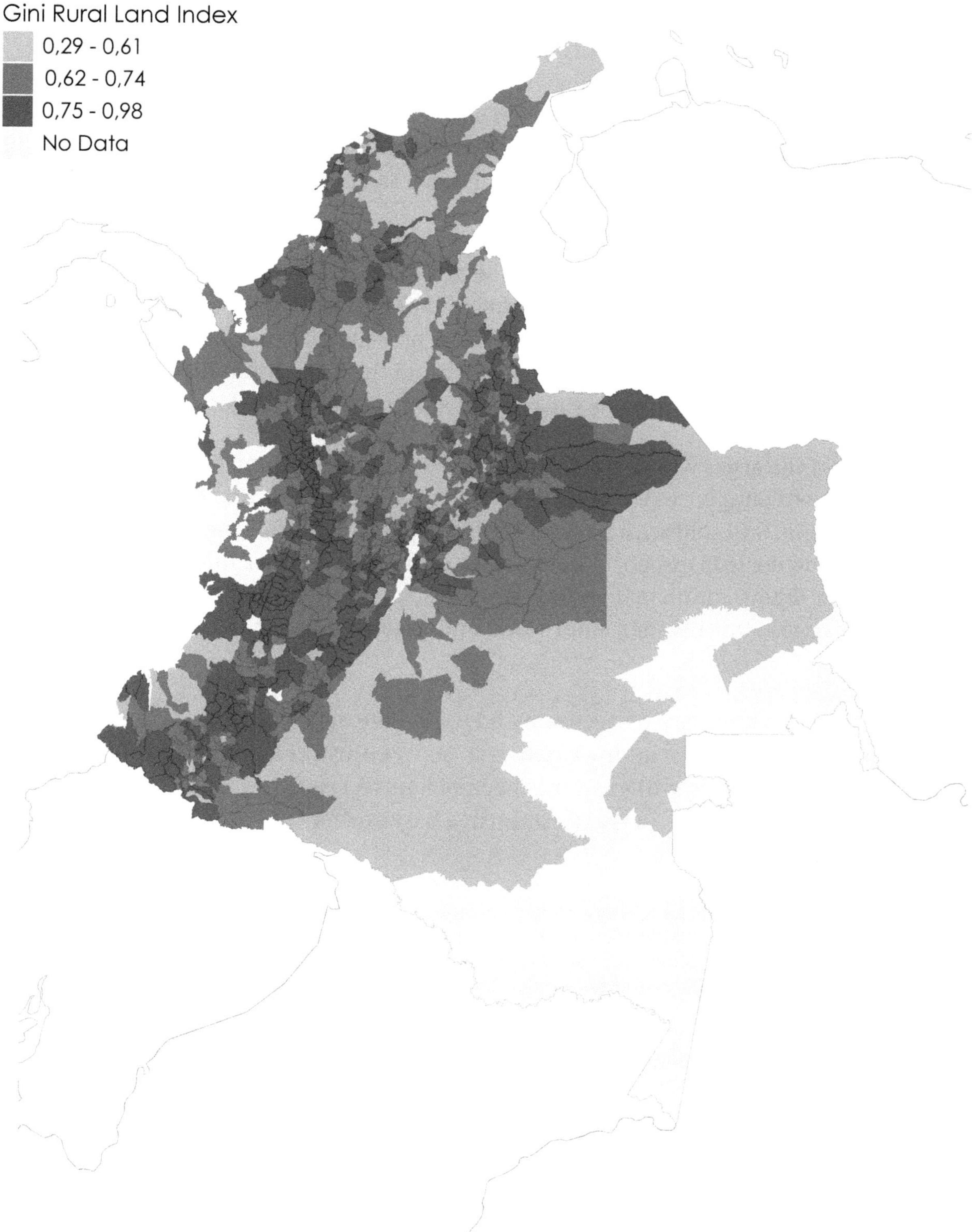

Source: UNDP Colombia National Human Development Report, 2009;
PNUD Informe Nacional de Desarrollo Humano Colombia, 2009.

massacres often paid for by, and killed on behalf of, large landowners seeking to protect their own interests.

The centrality of the issue was demonstrated by the agenda of the ongoing peace talks between the FARC and the government. The first point on the six-point agenda is land reform, and it remains the only point where there has been a general framework agreed to by both parties. While vague on specifics, the tentative agreement calls for a "radical" restructuring of rural Colombia, with priority being given to getting land and titles to landless peasants. One of the chief mechanisms for doing this would be the creation of the land bank called the Land Fund for Peace (*Fondo de Tierras Para la Paz*).[3] Another indication of how volatile the land issues remain was the series of crippling agricultural strikes from June through August that virtually shut down the country at times and caused the popularity of President Santos to plummet.[4]

The land titling and ownership issues remain the key bottlenecks in the consolidation of government's military gains in areas where it has cleared out the FARC and other non-state actors and seeks to establish a positive state presence. There can be no true citizen security until people have title to their property and the legal mechanisms to settle disputes. The thorniest issues predate the current administration by decades.

In many of the areas where the FARC has been the predominant force for decades, all land transactions simply ceased being recorded in the late 1950s. For five decades land was occupied, bought, and sold with no legal record of the transaction, meaning that there are no records of ownership, property boundaries, and a host of other information. In hundreds of other towns, municipal records were destroyed or lost during the conflict. In other cases landless peasants invaded empty land and began to farm, never holding title to it to begin with.

Because of this there are no accurate and up-to-date data available on land tenure.[5] The Santos government is undertaking a two-year "agricultural census," to be finished in 2014. The US$105 million study will examine the land tenure, crop production, and land usage in 3.8 million rural properties to try to establish a baseline for future actions. It is the first such undertaking since 1970.[6]

---

3. Patricia Grogg and Constanza Viera, "Key Land Reform Accord in Colombian Peace Talks," IPS, May 27, 2013, http://www.ipsnews.net/2013/05/key-land-reform-accord-in-colombias-peace-talks/. See also Christian Voelkel, "Three Reasons why Colombia's Land Reform Deal is Significant," International Crisis Group, May 28, 2013, http://www.crisisgroupblogs.org/crimeandpolitics/2013/05/28/three-reasons-why-colombias-land-reform-deal-is-significant/.

4. Arturo Wallace, "Paro Agrario: el momento más dificil del gobierno Santos," BBC News, September 5, 2013, http://www.bbc.co.uk/mundo/noticias/2013/09/130905_colombia_paro_agrario_encuesta_santos_popularidad_reeleccion_aw.shtml.

5. The most comprehensive study available at this time is a study done jointly by the national government and Universidad de Los Andes. Instituto Geográfico Agustín Codazzi (IGAC), *Atlas de la Distribución de la Propiedad Rural en Colombia* (Bogatá: IGAC/Imprenta Nacional de Colombia, 2012), http://otramiradadelconflicto.wikispaces.com/file/view/ATLAS+DE+LA+DISTRIBUCI%C3%93N+DE+LA+PROPIEDAD+RURAL+EN+COLOMBIA+-+IGAC.pdf/436399100/ATLAS%20DE%20LA%20DISTRIBUCI%C3%93N%20DE%20LA%20PROPIEDAD%20RURAL%20EN%20COLOMBIA%20-%20IGAC.pdf.

6. Natalia Herrera Durán and Alfredo Molano Jimeno, "En Colombia se hará un nuevo Censo National

A recent study by the United Nations Development Program (UNDP), using a series of research approaches and databases compiled by Universidad Los Andes, a respected Colombian university, concluded that Colombia has one of the most unequal land tenure patterns in Latin America, with just 1.5 percent of Colombians owning 52.2 percent of the land.

When inequality is measured using the Gini coefficient (a measure of inequality in which 1 represents the highest concentration of wealth, meaning that the higher the coefficient, the more concentrated the country's wealth), Colombia ranks at 0.86, indicating a dangerous concentration of land among a very few landholders.[7]

This extreme concentration of land in the hands of a very few, and the almost complete lack of attention to the issue over past decades, have given the FARC a political opening as the champion of landless peasants that it continues to exploit. Throughout the 1980s and 1990s the paramilitary groups, often supported by the military, began as groups paid by large landowners to defend their extensive rural properties, often taken by force from local communities.

The land acquisitions were possible because there was little state presence in much of the country. Wealthy individuals, drug barons, large agricultural businesses, or large landowners could simply pay local notary publics to put vast tracts of untitled land in their name, and then begin charging rent to anyone who lived on the newly "legalized" property. Often the only thing that changed hands was between the "purchaser" and the notary public, with those living without legal title finding themselves either forced from their homes or forced to pay to stay, a lucrative model that "was without risk and without investment."[8]

In the mid-1980s the leaders of the Medellín cartel, particularly Pablo Escobar and Gonzalo Rodriguez Gacha, bought up millions of acres of land in the Magdalena Medio region and greatly enhanced the paramilitary structures. With their unlimited resources they brought in Israeli and Australian mercenaries to provide the groups with training in military and intelligence procedures and the use of explosives and communications gear.

This land grab by the cartel leaders led the self-defense groups to transform themselves into a true military force and introduce themselves to drug-trafficking structures, which they later exploited to great benefit. It also brought a new level of savagery to the simmering land conflicts. The drug lords and their allies were better armed and equipped than the military (whom they often collaborated with), and better trained than the FARC. As the

---

Agropercuario," *El Espectador*, December 17, 2012, http://www.elespectador.com/noticias/politica/articulo-392957-colombia-se-hara-un-nuevo-censo-nacional-agropecuario.

7. Programa de las Naciones Unidas, para el Desarrollo (PNUD), *Colombia Rural: Razones para la Esperanza: Informe Nacional de Desarrollo Humano 2011* (Bogatá: PNUD, December 2011), http://hdr.undp.org/en/reports/national/latinamericathecaribbean/colombia/NHDR_Colombia_2011_ES_low.pdf.

8. This description is based on both the author's fieldwork and discussions with Alejandro Reyes, a leading expert on land tenure in Colombia. He described the model and used the cited phrase in the CSIS conference in Bogotá, Colombia, June 17, 2013.

predominant power in vast areas of the country, they could accuse anyone who opposed their land grabs of being FARC sympathizers, and thus began the systematic slaughter of civilians on a scale that far exceeded the earlier bloodshed.

During the mid-1990s the FARC gained considerable territorial control by providing protection to landless peasants migrating to Putumayo and other regions to take over vast tracts of land to grow coca, the raw material for cocaine. Over time the FARC amassed considerable revenue by taxing coca production and gaining control of cocaine laboratories and cocaine marketing structures; this enabled the FARC to purchase new weapons, recruit new members, and build a broad international network. As demonstrated in the recent agricultural strikes, the coca growers now claim hundreds of thousands of acres of land that has never been titled, surveyed, or legalized and are demanding state services for their ad hoc communities.

This cycle of violence, coupled with the internal conflict and constant fighting in economically prosperous banana regions, in turn drove millions of people from the countryside to urban areas. Food production dropped, unemployment rose, and the FARC found a fertile recruitment pool that allowed their clandestine structures to push ever closer urban centers, a longtime strategic goal.

In recent years, as paramilitaries have disbanded and lost their structural coherence—although many members drifted into criminal gangs—and government security forces have cleared increasingly more of the remote regions of the country, demands have become more acute for some sort of resolution to the intractable problems land titling.

The Santos government's response has two primary components. Both are costly and controversial, and it has been debated whether they are sustainable in the long term. Yet they represent the most sustained and comprehensive efforts in Colombia's history to find a long-term solution to a major root cause of much of the nation's unrest.

The first pillar is agricultural census, to establish a baseline of current data on land tenure and titling.

The second is the National Policy of Territorial Consolidation and Reconstruction (*Política Nacional de Consolidación y Reconstrucción Territorial*—PNCRT), the primary government mechanism for consolidating government presence in areas recently cleared by the military of nonstate armed actors. The program was begun under President Álvaro Uribe, Santos's predecessor, and was expanded considerably under the current administration.

The fundamental concept is to bring a "whole government" approach to regions that have been abandoned by the central government for decades, if not centuries. Every part of the government, from the administration of justice to education to public health to infrastructure is supposed to participate in the effort. At the heart of the effort, embedded with the joint task forces described in Chapter 3, are "units of territorial consolidation," including judges specially trained to adjudicate land disputes.

So far only 58 towns are covered under the program, with 82 more municipalities scheduled to be incorporated by the end of the year. These towns receive far more central government support than those outside the program, yet progress remains painstakingly slow on this issue because of the complexity, lack of records, and continued disputes. Yet even this limited plan, covering less than 13 percent of the nation's municipalities, will cost US$1.3 billion from 2012 to 2014.[9]

Even though the PNCRT is widely considered a positive step forward, leaders of civil society have criticized how it is being executed, the lack of coordination among different government agencies, the lack of coordination among the local and national government institutions, and overreliance on the military. Many of the remote towns have no electricity, poor roads that limit access, and relatively little communication with the outside world, complicating the tasks of setting up functioning state entities, and the military is providing the bulk of the engineering and logistical services.

Leaders of the program acknowledge that significant problems exist, particularly in coordinating efforts among government agencies and in meeting the felt needs of the community rather than just the strategic needs identified by the national government. However, they note that the program they are developing is new, with little international experience to draw from, and that in order to be successful multiple parts of the program have to be implemented simultaneously. Because of this the program is under constant evaluation and revision.[10]

Both critics and supporters of the program agree that the biggest challenge to the process over the long term is getting in place a credible judicial process whereby ownership of land that has been occupied can be legalized and where those who have been driven from their land can seek restitution.

Because so many millions of people have been driven from their land, the Santos administration has focused on an innovative program to provide restitution to millions of those displaced by the violence.

In June 2011 Santos signed into law the historic Victims and Land Restitution Law (*Ley de Víctimas y Restitución de Tierras*), which provides a hybrid judicial and administrative process designed to return millions of acres of land to some 4 million IDPs over 10 years' time. Human Rights Watch called the program "the most important human rights initiative of the Santos administration," explaining that if it is implemented effectively, "it will help thousands of families who have been devastated by the conflict to return home and rebuild their lives while undercutting the power of armed groups and criminal mafias."[11]

---

9. Fact sheet provided by the Colombian Ministry of Defense.

10. This information is based on author interviews in the Tolima area of consolidation as well as the comments made by civil society leaders and government officials at the CSIS conference in Bogotá, Colombia, June 17, 2013. Among the items most criticized were the *kit básico* or basic immediate projects that the plan provides.

11. Human Rights Watch, *The Risk of Returning Home.*

The Santos government created three institutions with national level presence for the implementation of this law. First among them is the Victims Unit, which provides humanitarian assistance to the conflict's victims, implements reparations, operates the Unified Victims' Registry, and coordinates the National System of Attention and Reparation. This unit has 95 offices across the country, with more than 2,000 employees. The second, the Land Restitution Unit, focuses on returning land to victims and operates the Registry of Dispossessed Lands, reversing the burden of proof by requiring current landholders to prove that their titles are legal. Finally, the Center for Historical Memory maintains archives of documents, testimonies, and research and directs construction of the National Museum of Memory in consultation with victims.

Passage of the law immediately raised expectations and brought a flood of applicants seeking to return to their homes, but the power of those occupying the land soon became apparent. The program has been very slow to get off the ground. As of September 17, 2013, only 700 cases of land restitution, for a total of 15,000 hectares—about 0.6 percent of the land in dispute—have been resolved by restitution judges. Of those cases, 66 percent of restitution beneficiaries have returned to live or work on their properties, 24 percent are waiting to return, and only 10 percent have not returned. A victim's decision to return to their land is voluntary, and 223 victim families have developed productive plans with the Land Restitution Unit.[12]

Many of those returning have been harassed, and a Human Rights Watch report documented numerous attacks and death threats against IDP land claimants and restitution leaders. For example, one of the leaders of the claimants, Iván Darío Restrepo, was gunned down in front of his wife and three children on May 4, 2013, after his police escorts had gone off duty.[13]

In many cases those who filed for restitution and were granted access to their land arrived only to find armed men there to keep them from taking possession of it. In some cases, using a favorite ploy of the FARC and paramilitary groups, anonymous "death lists" have been drawn up identifying the people who would be killed.[14]

As part of its program, the Colombian government's National Protection Unit (UNP) was created at the end of 2011 to replace the Ministry of the Interior's Protection Program. Today the UNP protects human rights defenders and victims of displacement, among others, with greater efficiency and impact—and with a significantly larger budget. The agency coordinates and enforces protection provisions for organizations and people whose lives have been threatened and are under extraordinary risk as a result of their rank or activities.

12. This information is based on "Victims and Land Restitution Law: Addressing the impact of Colombia's Internal Armed Conflict," fact sheet, Colombian Embassy, Washington, DC, October 2013.

13. "Reclamante de tierra Iván Darío Restrepo Garcia, asesinado en Bello, Antioquia el 4 de may," Comisión Intereclesial de Justicia y Paz, May 9, 2013, http://justiciaypazcolombia.com/Reclamante-de-Tierra-Ivan-Dario.

14. There is extensive media reporting on the threats received by land claimants and the ordeals they are facing. See, for example, "En Antioquia aumentan las amenazas contra los reclamantes de tierra," Caracol, June 27, 2013, http://www.caracol.com.co/noticias/regionales/en-antioquia-aumentan-las-amenazas-contra-los-reclamantes-de-tierras/20130706/nota/1911987.aspx.

In 2001 the program's budget was just US$7 million; in 2013 the full budget is US$140 million. As of October 17, 2013, more than 8,000 persons had special security measures in place, and the UNP continues to conduct security risk assessments in different parts of the country to ensure that anyone in need of special protection receives it.

The government, security forces, Attorney General's Office, Prosecutor General's Office, and UNP have established integrated intelligence centers to provide safety measures and draw risk assessment maps in the areas where victims have requested land restitution. The UNP coordinates and enforces protection provisions for organizations and people who have been threatened and are under elevated risk. As of June 2013 the National Protection Unit protected 500 land restitution leaders.

As the threats mounted against those seeking restitution, so did the threats against the specialized restitution judges. Several dozen of the judges wrote a letter to Santos requesting protection, noting that they were even more exposed to attacks than those seeking restitution because they "are the ones who order the legal and material restitution."

The Santos administration has been very vocal in denouncing the attacks on those seeking restitution and has been somewhat effective in providing security to those who receive death threats. Yet it has yet to bring charges against anyone issuing the threats or to prosecute any of the suspected perpetrators.

In a July 2012 speech, Santos identified the main perpetrators of the violence against the claimants, saying "many of the people making threats . . . are the owners or supposed owners of the pieces of land that have been reclaimed. . . . There are other sectors, sectors that I have called the extreme left . . . and the extreme right, who are linked to the old paramilitaries, who do not want the land they wrongfully appropriated to be taken away from them."[15]

The problems have persisted—in part, as human rights groups have pointed out, because the government's primary response to the violence has been high-level denunciations rather than actions to deal with the root of the problem. Many of the paramilitary groups were never completely dismantled, and because the rate of impunity for those involved in violence against claimants is so high, there is little risk to the perpetrators.

Yet even the critics of the policy acknowledge that Colombia is undertaking an immense task with few modern historic precedents for guidance. While still fighting a significant insurgency and multiple violent and well-armed nonstate actors, the state is attempting to simultaneously find solutions to the historic problem of land tenure and title at time when international aid for both efforts is declining.

Long-term success is far from guaranteed and will depend on multiple factors. One of the most important will be the government's ability to protect those who return to their

15. Quotation taken from Human Rights Watch, *The Risk of Returning Home*, p. 17.

Map 4. Land Restitution Requests

One of the landmark programs of the Santos administration is the Victims and Land Restitution Law, enacted in 2011. The law is intended to redress the historic displacement by illegal armed groups of millions of people from their land. This map shows the regions where displaced persons have filed for restitution, or the return of their land. While the program has been widely hailed by human rights groups, those seeking restitution often face violence or the threat of violence when they try to return home.

Number of land restitution applications per municipality

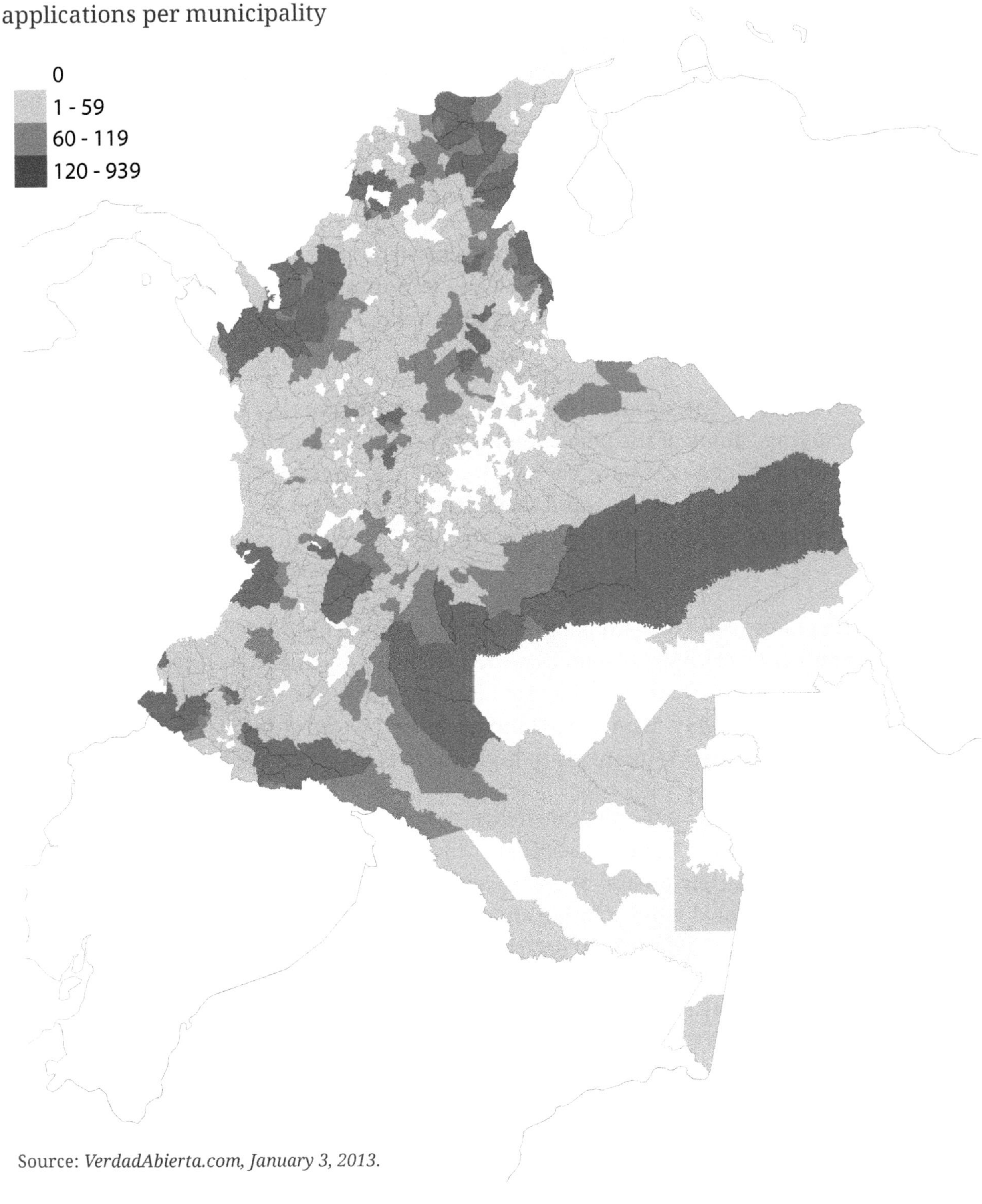

Source: *VerdadAbierta.com, January 3, 2013.*

land and to weaken the powerful groups that offer violent resistance to those efforts. Another key factor will be the ability to devise and implement a credible system of titling lands in regions where no documentation exists, few reliable land boundaries are demarcated, and multiple claims will likely be made for many properties. The titling and adjudication processes must be credible so that they will be seen as legitimate.

Finally, the programs will have to be supported, both financially and politically, for many years. Yet they must have an immediate impact, to keep people from becoming disillusioned and turning their backs on the programs. Such a loss of credibility would make reaching a viable solution much more difficult.

As in many countries, a change in the party in power brings a complete revamping of priorities and programs. In order to succeed, the programs of territorial consolidation and land restitution will need to be exempt from sharp swings in resourcing and goals. While programs constantly evolve and change with time, as with the overarching structure of Plan Colombia over the past 15 years, there must be fundamental continuity. Without that, the fragile gains of the past three years will disappear quickly and eradicating the roots of the violence will remain a distant dream.

5 | Resources: Access and Oversight

By Douglas Farah

Although to the outside world the violence in Colombia often appears to be driven almost entirely by drug trafficking, in fact the causes often center on other conflicts surrounding other resources. Drug trafficking is certainly an economic engine that has propelled Colombia to significant levels of violence and allowed the FARC, paramilitaries, and BACRIM to flourish. But it has also fed other conflicts that have simmered for decades.

Some of the resource conflicts that were at the forefront during the 1980s and 1990s, such as those surrounding oil and banana production, have waned as the state has reasserted its authority and presence. Attacks on oil pipelines, which in earlier decades were blown up hundreds of times a year by insurgents and cost millions of dollars in repairs and lost production, have dropped to fewer than a dozen last year.

Colombia is now Latin America's fourth largest oil producer, pumping about 1.1 million barrels of crude a day.[1]

Banana production in Urabá, particularly, was marred for decades by savage wars among the FARC, the AUC, and other groups. Union leaders and municipal leaders suspected of being sympathetic to the FARC were killed, often along with their families, by the paramilitaries. The FARC extorted, taxed, and kidnapped businessmen and landholders in the region and fought the AUC. The value of controlling the banana-producing land was shown when Chiquita Brands International was fined $25 million for paying $1.7 million in bribes to the AUC as well hundreds of thousands of dollars to the FARC in protection money as control of the territory shifted in the 1980s and 1990s.[2] Although problems still persist, the territory once in dispute is no longer a war zone.

But there is also a web of interrelated conflicts, often local or regional, surrounding many of Colombia's abundant natural resources, including minerals, rare earth metals,

1. Carlos Vargas, "Colombia Expects Higher Average Oil Production in 2013," Reuters, February 7, 2013, http://www.reuters.com/article/2013/02/07/colombia-energy-idUSL1N0B77KM20130207.

2. In the case Chiquita argued that it paid the money to the armed groups in order to protect the lives of its workers on the banana plantations. In 2004 the company sold its Colombia holdings, but still faces lawsuits totaling billions of dollars from Colombian family members of those killed by the armed groups. Chiquita has asked the suits be blocked. See Arthur Brice, "Chiquita Finding Bittersweet for Families of Men Killed in Colombia," CNN, February 12, 2010, http://www.cnn.com/2010/WORLD/americas/02/12/colombia.chiquita.farc/.

gemstones, and large-scale crops such as palm oil. These local and regional conflicts over resources, often ignored by the central government, are increasingly the cause of the more dispersed violence in Colombia and, if a peace process were reached, would likely be the centers of new criminal enterprises and the violence surrounding them.[3]

As Map 5 clearly shows, there is a strong correlation between resource extraction and areas with high levels of violence, including violence related to land issues. Armed groups compete for the resource "honeypots"—extractable, high-value commodities—which will in turn allow them to expand their power and control.

Due to state weakness, the illegal extraction of resources often not only provides a nonstate armed actor with revenue but also provides employment opportunities in regions where jobs are scarce, engendering local legitimacy for the armed group. This ability to simultaneously supplant a key government function (job creation) while financing a group or movement that owes no allegiance to the state, is a powerful part of the dynamic in Colombia's multiple internal conflicts and historic and chronic state weakness. The same dynamic holds true in areas where peasants have arrived by the thousands to cultivate coca crops and poppy for the making of cocaine and heroin.

"Ten years of the policy of Democratic Security has forced the FARC and ELN deep into the mountains and jungles, precisely where there has been the most growth in petroleum and mining activities," noted one report. "Because of this the map of the internal conflicts in Colombia and the map of mining and energy resources overlap, giving rise to new concerns about violence."[4]

One recent study identified bananas, coffee, emeralds, nickel, cut flowers, oil, and palm oil as resources that "are associated with armed conflict, either directly or indirectly, in different parts of the country."[5] Another study of illegal mining in Colombia found that the illicit extraction of gold had become a more important source of income than cocaine for the FARC and other groups in at least some provinces of significant conflict. In addition, as the price of an ounce of gold rose from $300 in 2003 to between $1,500 and $1,800 recently, more and more people are opting for gold mining rather than agricultural production or other jobs in the licit economy.

"Many believe that what the Colombian government calls the mineral-energy engine of the economy is good news," the report said. "But part of the problem is that illegal armed groups also think it is good for them."[6]

---

3. This argument is made persuasively in numerous academic studies and media reports. See Ralf Leiteritz, Carlo Nasi, and Angelika Rettberg, "Para desvincular los recursos naturales del conflicto armado en Colombia," *Colombia Internacional* 70 (July–December 2009): 215–229.

4. Frédéric Massé and Johanna Camargo, *Actores Armados Ilegales y Sector Extractivo en Colombia* (Madrid: Centro Internacional Toledo para la Paz [CITpax] and Observatorio Internacional, 2012), http://www.toledopax.org/uploads/Actores_armados_ilegales_sector_extractivo.pdf.

5. Leiteritz et al., "Para desvincular los recursos naturales del conflicto armado en Colombia."

6. Massé and Camargo, *Actores Armados Ilegales y Sector Extractivo en Colombia*.

Map 5. Illegal Mining in Colombia

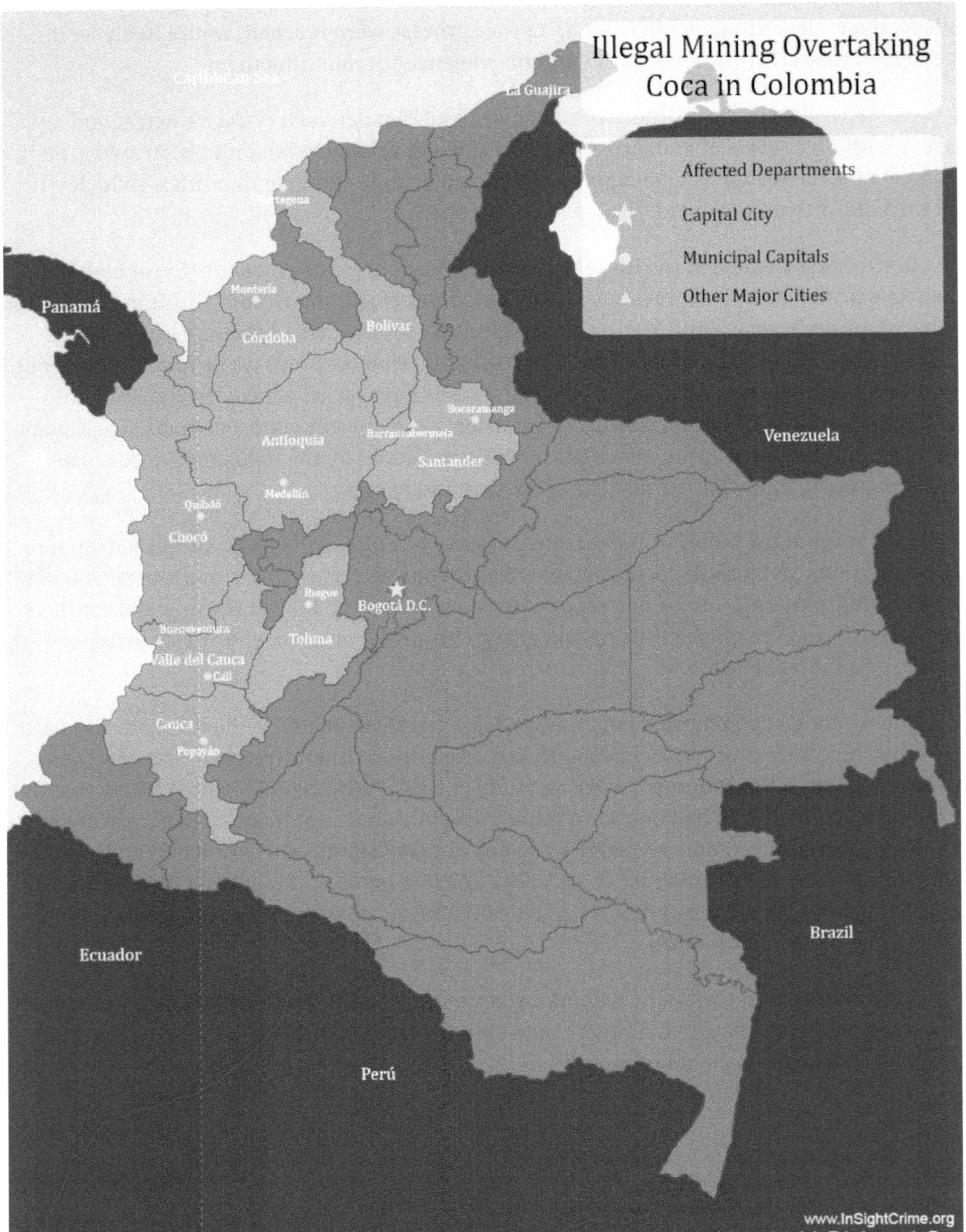

Note: This map is intended to show, in general terms, the extent to which extralegal mining takes place throughout Colombia's territory. This is indicated on a department-by-department basis, and the uniformity of shading within each department does not imply an even distribution of extralegal mining activity.

Several studies of the exploitation of natural resources in Colombia note that the practice of small-scale mining without license from the state dates back centuries and has seldom been dealt with as an illicit activity, even though it is against the law. Rather, it is tolerated as way for isolated, rural inhabitants to make a living.

While the state in theory is the sole legitimate buyer of the mined ores, the state is often absent. It is easier and tax-free in these "ungoverned spaces" for miners to move the products across a border to another country or simply sell the ore to legal miners, who can mix the product in with the legal product.

So what is new is not the illicit extraction of resources, but the scale on which it is currently happening and who the beneficiaries are. Some studies find that the illicit mining sector is mining half of Colombia's wealth in some minerals, such as gold, emeralds, and coltan. In addition to depriving the state of significant revenue from taxes, the miners in the informal sector are causing enormous ecological damage through the use of chemicals, primarily mercury, to extract the minerals; these chemicals then are put directly back into formerly pristine waterways.[7]

The traditional attitude toward artisanal mining is rooted in the concept that the activity takes place in an "ungoverned" space where the inhabitants operate in a power vacuum. The concept of "ungoverned spaces" has gained currency in policy and academic circles, but it does not accurately reflect the reality on the ground in many places such as Colombia.[8] Rather, in almost every part of Colombia (and in the vast majority of the world's conflict zones), although the state is absent there is a group or force that exercises some form of government.[9] In many remote areas of Colombia, particularly in resource-rich regions, the FARC or other groups are the real power and the state is absent. But the absence of the state does not translate into a lack of governance, it is simply a multiplicity of alternative sources of governance that all serve to weaken the Colombian state.

There are multiple advantages to nonstate armed actors exploiting resources other than cocaine today. While the overall market for cocaine in the United States dropped by 40 percent from 2006 and 2012,[10] coca cultivators and their coca fields have been under persistent pressure from the Colombian government. As a result, coca production in Colombia dropped from a high of 78,000 hectares (198,120 acres) in 2006 to 48,000 hectares (121,920 acres) in 2012, and the number of people making their living from coca dropped by a third.

---

7. Agencia EFE, "La minería illegal en Colombia alcanza el 50% de la extracción total del país," November 22, 2011, http://www.google.com/hostednews/epa/article/ALeqM5ippyn90Smlsq6nXj6EsCx1HkLRBg?docId=1659786&hl=es.

8. See, for example, Angel Rabasa et al., *Ungoverned Territories: Understanding and Reducing Terrorism Risks* (Santa Monica, CA: RAND, 2007), http://www.rand.org/content/dam/rand/pubs/monographs/2007/RAND_MG561.pdf.

9. For a fuller explanation of this concept, see Douglas Farah, *Transnational Organized Crime, Terrorism, and Criminalized States in Latin America*. (Carlisle, PA: Strategic Studies Institute, U.S. Army War College, September 2012) http://www.strategicstudiesinstitute.army.mil/pubs/display.cfm?pubID=1117.

10. Stacy Teicher Khadaroo, "Cocaine Use: Will the Steady Decline Continue?" *Christian Science Monitor*, July 12, 2013, http://www.csmonitor.com/USA/Society/2013/0712/Cocaine-use-Will-the-factors-behind-its-steady-decline-continue.

Bolivia and Peru have picked up much of the slack, but the shrinking market to the north and shifting coca cultivation to the south represent a dramatic shift the dynamics of the cocaine trade away from Colombia as the center of gravity.[11]

This has forced nonstate armed actors, particularly the FARC and several major BACRIM groups, to look for other sources of revenue. One of the primary venues now being developed is illicit or unlicensed mining in gold, tungsten, coltan, and other minerals. This presents far less risk for both those carrying out the mining and those controlling the mining activities. While cocaine trafficking is viewed as a priority for international law enforcement and carries long jail sentences upon conviction, illicit minerals and ores are both easy to blend into the legal economy and carry far lighter sentences if detected.

There is another huge advantage to illegal groups, particularly with gold. A 2011 report on gold mining found that although the state is the sole legal buyer of mineral products, only 14 percent of the 53 tons of gold mined in Colombia—of which 98 percent was exported—were legally extracted. The report noted several significant anomalies in Colombia's gold exports and concluded that gold exports are part of "a giant black hole where there is a mix of money laundering, corruption, benefits for illegal armed groups and the opportunism of some local authorities who offer a cloak of legitimacy to a gigantic laundering operation of illicit resources."[12]

The report found that in many of the municipalities reporting surging gold bonanzas, no gold was ever really mined. Rather, municipal officials and gold brokers, who issue export licenses for gold exports, have run elaborate scams that allow drug traffickers and other nonstate actors to legitimize their drug profits as gold exports. A separate report by the National Ombudsman's Office (*Defensoría del Pueblo*) also found that small-scale illegal gold mining was used extensively to launder money for the FARC, BACRIM, and other groups.[13]

Despite the use of gold and other commodities to launder money, there is an undeniable growth in mining activities, both licit and illicit. In most cases the armed groups tax the equipment and production of the illegal mines, rather than carry out the mining themselves. The taxes run up to 20 percent of production as well as taxes per unit of heavy equipment brought in for the work. In other cases the FARC or other groups act as brokers, buying the mined ore, bundling it into larger shipments, and moving it for sale on the international market.

---

11. UNODC, "Colombia: Coca Cultivation Survey 2012." http://www.unodc.org/documents/crop-monitoring/Colombia/Colombia_Coca_Cultivation_Survey_2012_web.pdf.

12. "La nueva lavandería," *Revista Dinero*, September 6, 2011, http://www.dinero.com/caratula/edicion-impresa/articulo/la-nueva-lavanderia/120971.

13. Volmar Antonio Pérez Ortiz et al., *Minería de Hecho en Colombia* (Bogatá: Defensoría del Pueblo, December 2010), http://www.defensoria.org.co/red/anexos/publicaciones/mineriaColombia.pdf.

In addition to gold, a long-standing problem now exacerbated by the confluence of factors described above, illicit mining under the protection of armed groups is branching out into new minerals that have a high market value.

Among these are tungsten, coltan, and tantalum. All are minerals now used in new car engines, computers, microchips, smartphones, and other electronic devices. Until a decade ago these minerals did not command a high enough price to make the backbreaking work of extracting them from remote jungle regions worth the effort.

However, with the surge in new technologies increasing demand and the Chinese buying and storing these strategic minerals across the globe, demands for alternative sources have surged in recent years. The FARC particularly is active in tungsten mining, both paying peasants to mine the ore from riverbeds and running its own large mining operation on a jungle hilltop called Tiger Hill (*Cerro El Tigre*) in the southeast corner of Colombia where the borders of Colombia, Brazil, and Venezuela touch. They can reportedly mine 15 metric tons of wolframite, or tungsten ore, per week.[14]

Despite the significant gains made by the Colombian military against the FARC in recent years (see Chapter 3 on security), Tiger Hill remains out of their reach, allowing the FARC to carry out its lucrative mining activities where moving the ore across the border is relatively easy, particularly to Venezuela, where the government is friendly to the FARC.

The Tiger Hill mine illustrates much of the harm this type of mining can do. In addition to funding a guerrilla movement designated as a terrorist organization by the United States and the European Union, it is taking place in the Puinawai National Forest, part of a reserve that is supposed to be a protected habitat for an indigenous community. The deforestation and runoff from the mining activity are spoiling the nearby Inirida River, and those Puinawai who do not want to mine or who oppose the FARC are driven from their land or killed.

"It is completely illegal, but we haven't been able to stop it yet," Colonel Luis Montenegro, the National Police commander of Guainia Province, told Bloomberg News. "We don't control any territory out there, FARC controls it."

Coltan, known as a conflict mineral in Africa, where resource wars have broken out in the Democratic Republic of Congo, is mined in the same national park, and its path to market is even more convoluted, touching every major illicit actor in the region.

FARC guerrillas control the mining area of the coltan, a mineral used in smartphones and computer screens, and charge miners before they can dig. Former paramilitary bands control the route that miners must traverse with woven baskets full of rocks, weighing up

---

14. For a detailed account of the Tiger Hill mining operation and illegal activities in the surrounding areas, see Michael Smith, "How Colombian FARC Terrorist Mining Tungsten Are Linked to Your BMW Sedan," *Bloomberg Markets Magazine*, August 8, 2013, http://www.bloomberg.com/news/2013-08-08/terrorist-tungsten-in-colombia-taints-global-phone-to-car-sales.html.

to 50 pounds, and they have to be paid off on every trip. It is unavoidable because the brokers demand that the ore be delivered outside the national park, where penalties for being caught are far less.[15]

Colombian police said some of the illicit mining operations around Puinawai National Park were run by members of the Cifuentes Villa family.[16] The U.S. Treasury Department's Office of Foreign Assets Control (OFAC) put the a dozen members of the Cifuentes Villa clan on the list of designated major drug kingpins, alleging they ran a cocaine trafficking and money laundering that worked closely with Joaquin "El Chapo" Guzman, the leader of the Mexican-based Sinaloa cartel and one of the most powerful drug traffickers in the world.[17]

While the illegal mining is posing a major challenge to the Colombian government's strategy of cutting the FARC and other armed groups off from financial resources, there are other significant problems surrounding access to resources and access to them. Many date back many years and are directly related to land tenure issues.

One of the primary problems of ongoing concern is the monoculture production of African palm, to use as palm oil. Because the crop is an alternative, renewable fuel as well as a product used in hundreds of products, from soap to cosmetics, the government is promoting its expansion. However, to be economically viable it requires huge tracts of land surrounding a processing plant.

This led to multiple cases of entire communities, particularly the Afro-Caribbean communities in Urabá and Chocó, being driven from their land by large entrepreneurs who wanted the land to be cleared and planted for African palm production. Many of the groups who have driven the communities came directly from the former paramilitary structures. By some estimates 80 percent of the land under cultivation for African palm has serious legal challenges.[18] The Colombian state has taken several significant steps to return confiscated lands to their rightful owners. (See Chapter 4 on land tenure.)

One of the most comprehensive studies on the human rights impact of African palm cultivation was conducted in 2006 by a team of nongovernment organizations. The study found:

---

15. Ignacio Gómez, "Colombia's Black-Market Coltan Tied to Drug Traffickers, Paramilitaries," International Consortium of Investigative Journalists, March 4, 2012, http://www.publicintegrity.org/2012/03/04/8284/colombia-s-black-market-coltan-tied-drug-traffickers-paramilitaries.

16. Ibid.

17. Office of Foreign Assets Control, "Cifuentes Villa Drug Trafficking Organization," U.S. Department of Treasury, February 2011, http://www.treasury.gov/resource-center/sanctions/Programs/Documents/cifuentes_villa_ind_022011.pdf.

18. For a more comprehensive look at how the paramilitary AUC and its subsequent offspring moved heavily into African palm production, see Emily Harwell, Douglas Farah, and Arthur G. Blundell, *Forests, Fragility and Conflict: Overview and Case Studies* (Washington, DC: Program on Forests, June 2011), 67–11, http://www-wds.worldbank.org/external/default/WDSContentServer/WDSP/IB/2012/06/05/000427087_20120605094522/Rendered/PDF/693170ESW0P1200757000FRAGILE0FOREST.pdf.

> There is clearly a high level of causality between forced displacement and land theft, and between land theft and palm production. In all palm complexes there has been forced displacement and in all of them there are cases of illegal appropriation of land.[19]

The pressures to seize land may be exacerbated by the government policy of greatly expanding African palm cultivation and increasing production. Palm oil production has almost doubled over the past decade, from 527 metric tons in 2003 to a projected 1,000 metric tons in 2013.[20]

As the Colombian government extends its control to more distant regions of the country, it will need to prioritize bringing a significant state presence to areas of mineral resources and conflict. The illicit exploitation of gold, coltan, tungsten, and other minerals is a vital economic lifeline for criminal groups and insurgents. Bringing a positive state presence to cut off that flow of revenue and establish state legitimacy, perhaps for the first time in those areas, will be a challenge that must be met to overcome the cycle of violence.

---

19. Fidel Mingorance, *The Flow of Palm Oil Colombia-Belgium/Europe: A Study from a Human Rights Perspective* (Brussels: Human Rights Everywhere and Coordinacion Belge Pour la Colombie, November 2006), http://www.cbc.collectifs.net/doc/informe_en_v3-1.pdf.

20. Index Mundi, "Colombia Palm Oil Production by Year," http://www.indexmundi.com/agriculture/?country=co&commodity=palm-oil&graph=production.

6 Infrastructure Needs

By Douglas Farah

One of the biggest obstacles for extending state presence in Colombia has been the historic lack of infrastructure to tie the nation together. Colombia's geography is a major factor: the vast majority of the population is centered in three mountain ranges, and lightly populated expanses of Amazon jungle and tropical forests make up almost half the national territory.

Insurgencies and paramilitary groups prospered in areas where the state was absent. In these isolated regions, the alternative governance systems that developed had no interest in constructing an economic infrastructure to integrate them with the state, and the violence and lack of political will kept the state from trying very hard to change the dynamic.

This combination of factors has led to Colombia's "monumental backwardness" in roads, ports, waterway development, and other critical infrastructure, according to Juan Martín, the president of Colombian Infrastructure Chamber. Despite its emerging market status, Colombia has an infrastructure that ranked only 79th among the 139 nations evaluated by the World Economic Forum.[1]

Like many of the problems Colombia faces moving forward, beginning to solve the complex and multifaceted infrastructure crisis will be costly, time consuming, and politically challenging. And like the myriad other challenges discussed in this chapter, the infrastructure deficit has its origins in the history of the country's development from colonial times and the internal conflicts of the past 50 years.

Under president Álvaro Uribe, defeating the guerrillas and clearing the existing transportation routes was a priority, with few resources available for expansion. Beginning in 1996 the FARC launched a highly successful campaign to control sections of the major highways leading to the nation's main cities. Until then the FARC had largely been deemed a rural problem and only an irritant for the urban elites, who were seldom inconvenienced by the conflict.

1. "Colombia's Infrastructure: Bridging the Gaps," *The Economist*, September 17, 2011, http://www.economist.com/node/21529036.

That changed when the FARC began to regularly set up armed roadblocks on the limited number of major highways and exact tolls on all vehicles passing through. The FARC used these roadblocks—*pescas milagrosas*, or miraculous fishing expeditions—which often lasted for hours before the army would show up, to capture wealthy people, whom they abducted and held for ransom. Freedom to travel was drastically curtailed. The situation deteriorated to the point where the military and police had to organize armed convoys to escort caravans of vehicles from one city to another, and virtually the only other way to move around the country was by air.

Beginning in 2002 Uribe made the safety of the road network a priority and slowly succeeded in making the road system fairly safe. Now, as the Colombian military has pushed back the nonstate armed groups and seeks to recoup vast swaths of national territory, remedying the backwardness of the long-neglected transportation infrastructure is one of the government's highest priorities.

Not only is infrastructure development viewed as key to economic growth, the lack of infrastructure is one of the primary social grievances against the government in areas where the state is seeking to reestablish its authority. Providing at least some of that infrastructure in a relatively short period of time is viewed as a key to undermining support for the FARC and other armed groups. In author visits to Tolima and Casanare Provinces, by far the highest priority for the local population was the construction of roads in order to move produce to market and have access to goods and services.

To meet these needs, the Santos government has announced the most ambitious infrastructure agenda the country has ever seen. His plan calls for US$55 billion in investments over 10 years, with about half the money coming from the private sector. The program, under the auspices of the recently created National Infrastructure Agency (*Agencia Nacional de Infraestructura*—ANI), will double the mileage of the nation's divided highways, improve airports, revive railroads, and upgrade the nation's extensive waterways for shipping by boat.

Such investment is desperately needed. For example, currently only two-lane highways link Medellín, the second largest city and industrial hub, to the Pacific and Caribbean coasts. The new plan calls for four connector highways from Medellín, including 540 miles of new road, 600 bridges, and 131 tunnels.

A World Bank report said it was significantly more expensive to ship products from the capital of Bogotá to the Caribbean coast that it was to ship products from the port of Cartagena to Shanghai. A national business association estimated that the lack of, or poor quality of, infrastructure added costs and delays equivalent to a 10 to 15 percent tax.[2]

2. William Moore, "Colombia's 'Infrastructure Blues,'" *The City Paper* (Bogotá), July 16, 2013, http://thecitypaperBogotá.com/business/colombias-infrastructure-blues/.

For the new infrastructure program to work, the government has had to clean up one of the other endemic problems that has slowed progress — corruption. This is something the Santos government is working hard to overcome in infrastructure projects through a series of measures designed to increase transparency. Among the measures the government has taken is the disbanding the notoriously corrupt Institute of Concessions (*Instituto de Concesiones*—INCO), which had been in charge granting infrastructure concessions, and reorganizing the ministry of transportation.[3]

In one notorious example of corruption, the consortium hired to build a key stretch of road between Bogotá and Girardot included a firm whose three principal owners are currently in jail on fraud, bribery, and other charges. The 75-mile project was supposed to be finished in 2011 but is now scheduled to be completed by the end of 2013.[4]

One report early this year noted:

> Political appointees infiltrated both entities, and were sometimes recommended by the very concessionaries whom they were responsible to supervise. Between 2002 and 2008, eight out of nine INCO directors found themselves in jail or in court.
>
> Political patronage and clientelism were compounded by general ineptitude. The Ministry of Transport would oversee open-bidding processes before issuing studies to estimate the cost of the projects and their associated risks during the construction process. Winning parties habitually renegotiated their contracts to obtain greater public resources, to reduce the size of their projects, and to lengthen periods of concessions. Worse still, the model permitted companies to receive payment prior to any construction.[5]

In place of INCO, the government created ANI, a government agency in charge of planning, structuring, coordinating, executing, managing, and evaluating infrastructure concessions. The government also closed many loopholes of the previous concessions process. The Santos administration also passed legislation to develop a modern Public-Private Partnership (PPP) regulatory framework to stimulate the participation of the private sector, not only in building the projects but in maintaining them going forward. Most concessions are for 30 years.

How well ANI works in both coordinating the necessary projects among different government agencies and keeping the bidding and construction processes transparent and on budget will go a long way toward determining whether Colombia can successfully sustain its economic growth.

---

3. Olivia Gagan and Vanessa Buendía, "IJ Infrastructure Investment Guide: Colombia," *IJ Infrastructure Journal*, June 2012, http://ppp.worldbank.org/public-private-partnership/sites/ppp.worldbank.org/files/documents/infrastructure-report_colombia.pdf.
4. "Colombia's Infrastructure: Bridging the Gaps," *The Economist*.
5. Moore, "Colombia's 'Infrastructure Blues.'"

Figure 1. ANI's Organization for Transportation Infrastructure

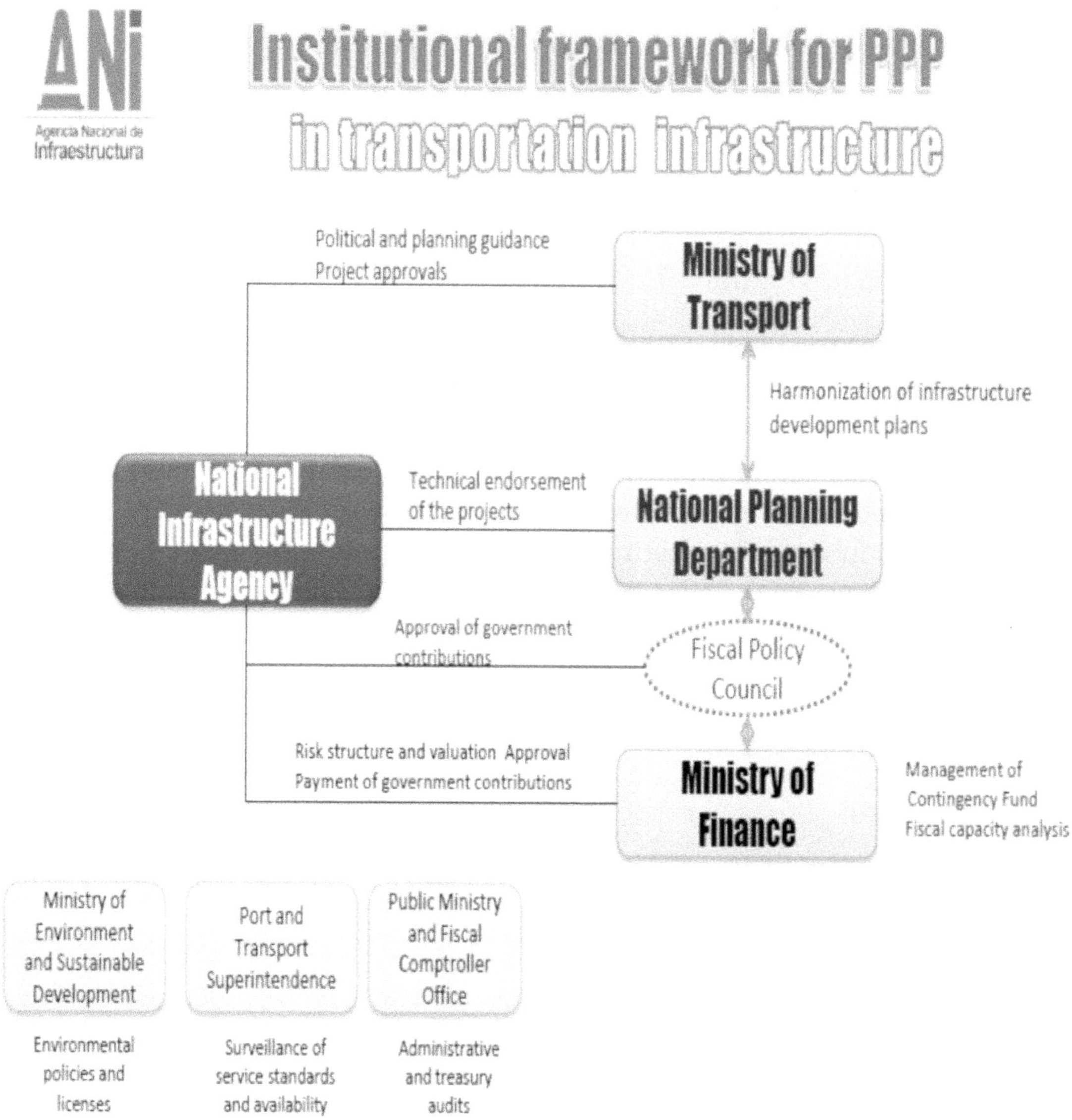

Source: PowerPoint presentation by Luis Fernando Andrade, ANI president, March 2013, provided by the Colombian Embassy in Washington, D.C.

In addition to US$25 billion in road projects, the Santos government plans on spending billions of dollars on dredging more than 500 miles of the Magdalena River to restore the waterway's place as one of the nation's main commercial arteries. Accessible from both Bogotá and Medellín, the river flows through the oil fields of the Llanos and Magdalena basins to the port of Barranquilla on the Caribbean coast.

The investment in dredging the river could quintuple the amount of river traffic, easing road congestion and speeding products to the Caribbean coast. A single large barge can carry the same amount of cargo as some 70 tractor-trailer trucks, making riverine transport both quicker and more efficient. In addition to dredging the Magdalena and other rivers and building a series of riverine ports, the national plan also contemplates building nine new privately run ports on the coast to increase foreign commerce.[6]

In addition to the roads and riverine building projects, the Santos government plans on modernizing other areas of infrastructure. Overall, from 2011 to 2018 the government projects expanding operational railroad lines from 508 miles to 1,412 miles; increasing port capacity from 132 million tons to 254 million tons; and increasing air passenger capacity from 20 million to 34 million.[7]

Over the past decade, despite the incredible obstacles, the Colombian economy has consistently outperformed the average GDP growth for both Latin America and the world. In 2011 Colombia's economy grew by 6.6 percent while the world averaged 3.2 percent.[8] This growth is all the more remarkable given the fact that the nation's transportation infrastructure is many decades out of date. The push by the Santos government, as large as it seems, is really just a first step in meeting Colombia's needs for the twenty-first century. If corruption is kept at bay and the expected foreign direct investment flows in, Colombia will be nothing short of transformed over the next decade.

6. Power Point presentation by Luis Fernando Andrade, ANI president, March 2013, provided by the Colombian Embassy in Washington, D.C; and Ramzy Bameih, "Monumental Backwardness Moving Forwards: Oil Production Demands Better Infrastructure in Colombia," Global Business Reports, June 19, 2013, http://gbroundup.com/2013/06/19/monumental-backwardness-moving-forwards-oil-production-demands-better-infrastructure-in-colombia/.

7. Gagan and Buendía, "IJ Infrastructure Investment Guide," 24.

8. Ibid., 9.

7 | Governance

By Robert D. Lamb

The insurgency in Colombia began 49 years ago and over the course of nearly five decades has involved leftist guerrillas, anti-guerrilla paramilitaries, organized criminals, narcotraffickers, and other conflict actors as well as the state security forces. Two decades ago, after the leftist guerrillas lost their main patron when the Soviet Union fell, the lines between left and right, licit and illicit, and state and nonstate became increasingly blurred, as combatants fighting for political motivations sought new sources of profit in narcotrafficking and extortion and those fighting for a profit motive saw opportunity in allying with battle-hardened fighters. In the 1990s, human rights violations were rampant, many government officials and security personnel were threatened or corrupted, the state's war against guerrillas was being fought in part by proxies that could not be controlled, and the guerrillas looked to be winning the war in large swaths of territory throughout the country. President Pastrana went so far as to agree to a cease-fire in a large, guerrilla-controlled territory while they pursued peace talks. As it became clear that the guerrillas were taking advantage of the cease-fire to regroup and were offering no credible counterproposals, those talks failed, and public cynicism about both sides in the conflict reached a peak.

Meanwhile, some key players in the Colombian military recognized that their strategy was not helping them win the counterinsurgency but was contributing to a growing disillusionment with the state. With support from some of their civilian counterparts and strong encouragement and support from the United States, the military began a process of introspection and professionalization in the late 1990s. By the early 2000s, this transformation had begun to pay dividends, as the military began to defeat guerrillas on the battlefield, starting with the region surrounding Bogotá in 2004, and the state suddenly found itself present in more and more territory it had not controlled in four decades.

In those areas, the main challenge suddenly changed. It was not simply how to beat insurgents, but rather how to govern newly liberated communities. Some in those communities had relatives fighting on the side of the guerrillas. Others were bitter at what they perceived as being the state's decades-long abandonment. Most hoped for peace.

In 2007, the government of Colombia launched the Integrated Consolidation Plan of Macarena, or PCIM (for Plan de Consolidación Integral de la Macarena), to begin establishing the state's civilian presence in six municipalities in southern Meta Department, to the south of Bogotá, near national parks in and around the Macarena mountain range. A special body in the president's office, the Center for the Coordination of Integrated Action (Centro de Coordinación de Acción Integral, or CCAI), took the lead in coordinating different government agencies and international donors to carry out the project. It was a fairly weak body, but its work managed to become a proof of concept.

By 2009, PCIM was succeeding in disrupting the cultivation of illicit crops (a funding source for guerrillas), strengthening the state's security presence, and bringing in civilian agencies to provide services. A study of the program undertaken that year observed:

> PCIM embodies what appears to be an important shift in the government of Colombia's hitherto not fully coordinated approach to establishing effective state presence in areas formerly controlled by illegal armed groups. As a strategy for consolidation of sustained state authority, PCIM's emphasis on rapid and sequenced action coordinated on an interagency basis has much potential for success not only in the Macarena but as a pilot project for use in other areas of Colombia.[1]

By the end of 2009, PCIM had become the model for Colombia's National Consolidation Plan (Plan Nacional de Consolidación, or PNC). In that plan, government agencies would enter cleared territories in sequence: first the military would clear insurgents, then police would eradicate coca crops, and finally civilian agencies would provide services. The objective was to make as much of a positive difference in the lives of the communities as possible as quickly as possible to give the communities confidence in the state's ability and willingness to govern them as citizens and not as guerrilla suspects. The PCIM model was expanded to departments of Tolima and Montes de Maria while continuing in Meta.

These programs were intended to gain local support for long-term stability efforts. By encouraging community participation in municipal development, the government of Colombia simultaneously worked to combat apathy while also instilling a sense of local ownership in achieving success. Government representatives encouraged residents to prioritize aid projects and provide feedback on design and implementation. The projects that were most successful at producing positive assessments of government efficiency and transparency were high-visibility infrastructure projects such as road and bridge repairs, school renovations, and access to energy.

The initial programs revealed a number of challenges that would need to be addressed if consolidation were to succeed: addressing local desires for permanent solutions and pacifying concerns that development projects would provide only short-term solutions; rooting political and legal institutions in local society so residents have faith the government will not abandon them; preventing disillusionment by meeting rising expectations for the central government's ability to meet local needs in development aid projects; and combating potential backsliding due to competing government priorities, changes in

1. Peter DeShazo, Phillip McLean, and Johanna Mendelson Forman, *Colombia's Plan de Consolidacion Integral de la Macarena: An Assessment* (Washington, DC: CSIS, June 2009), 12–13, http://csis.org/files/publication/090602_DeShazo_PCIM_Web.pdf.

administration, ongoing security challenges, or weak municipal government. An evaluation of the program identified several critical areas that needed to be addressed if the program were to be expanded:

- *Judicial reform*. The court system suffered from staff shortages, in part due to restructuring efforts aimed at combating historical incompetence and corruption. Judges were targeted by criminal actors and required bolstered security. And the consolidation programs would increase demand for specialized legal services to handle emerging land and property right issues.
- *Municipal authority*. Because the consolidation program was a national program, there was a risk that success would improve the state's legitimacy at the national but not the local level. The national government's ability to deliver goods and services would be diluted as the number of consolidation zones would increase in the future, so local institutions ould need to become self-sufficient. Mayors and Regional Consolidation Centers (RCCs) needed to serve as the main formalized structures connecting various government and nongovernment components, and the central government would need to ensure adequate funds and staff to support their development.
- *Public messaging*. As life improved in urban centers, where the most powerful political constituencies live, there was a risk that most Colombians would not understand the importance of rural consolidation. The government needed to communicate the benefits of its achievements while also identifying persistent challenges to get the resources needed to meet stated goals.
- *Land restitution*. Even with the FARC out of target zones, other illegal actors threatened tenuous stability and risked disrupting efforts to return displaced farmers to their land. In addition to the need to establish local police forces to prevent criminal activity and eradicate illegal sources of income, there needed to be real efforts to determine land ownership and improve support to commercial agricultural so that legal productive enterprises could be profitable. It was recognized that there was a need for legal titling reforms and crop substitution in national consolidation efforts.

In 2010, President Santos carried out a review of the consolidation programs and incorporated the PNC into his National Development Plan (Plan Nacional de Desarrollo, or PND). His concern was both to capture the lessons from the pilot effort on the issues described above (and others) and to institutionalize the overall consolidation concept, which otherwise was at risk of being a special project, separate from the normal institutions of development and administration, that would be abandoned in future administrations as political priorities changed.

The following year and partly as a result of that review, President Santos supported several important initiatives. One was the Victims and Land Restitution Law, signed in June 2011, to establish a system to return land to people who had been displaced during Colombia's conflicts and provide other benefits to victims. The other was a governmental reorganization that merged responsibility for consolidation and reconciliation work into a new Department for Social Prosperity. In that department a special Administrative Unit for Land Consolidation (Unidad Administrativa para la Consolidación Territorial, or UACT) was established to continue implementing the consolidation program, now called the National Policy of Territorial Consolidation and Reconstruction Policy (Política Nacional de Consolidación y Reconstrucción Territorial, or PNCRT).

The PNCRT is an ambitious effort, affecting more territories and mixing security and immediate-impact projects with longer-term initiatives to better integrate consolidation zones into the political, social, and economic life of the country. It relies on national agencies, international donors, and private-sector support to continue bringing security and civilian government institutions to newly liberated zones throughout Colombia. The PNCRT is intended to be a comprehensive approach with collaboration between national and local authorities, as well as civil society organizations. A participant in a recent workshop to discuss the program called it a "good step toward rebuilding civil society, providing a sense of ownership in its own reconstruction process."[2]

But the program still has a number of challenges to overcome:

- *Rule of law.* Courts still lack capacity to prosecute criminal activity and resolve land disputes. Moreover, the country's overall situation worsened between 2011 and 2012, with its rule-of-law score changing from –0.29 to –0.39 in the World Bank's Worldwide Governance Index. Even still, that places Colombia fourth in the region in the quality of rule of law, just below Uruguay, Chile, and Suriname.[3]
- *Access to basic services.* While development projects have increased the number of roads and opened transit routes between rural and urban areas, many locals still struggle to afford basic goods and services. Vulnerable populations such as ethnic minorities, women, and children are disproportionately affected (see Chapter 8 on social inclusion).
- *Local-national coordination.* Communication between the national government and local authorities remains weak. Some areas have no clear role for governors and mayors or lack a strategy for sustaining local governance.
- *Public communication.* Large segments of the populations, especially those who live in urban areas, still do not know what the consolidation plan is or how it affects them, putting the program's political support (and future funding) at risk.
- *Sustainability.* Transition initiatives are often unfairly accused of being short-term fixes or "band-aid" solutions. It is true that an important purpose of consolidation programs is to offer immediate benefits to boost the state's credibility with local populations. But it is also important to initiate longer-term programs to address root causes of conflict, which Colombia's consolidation program recognizes. There is

2. CSIS conference, Bogotá, June 2013.
3. World Bank, "Worldwide Governance Indicators," http://info.worldbank.org/governance/wgi/index.aspx#reports.

concern, however, that implementation of longer-term projects might be sacrificed to changing priorities or might not have the funding needed. Many development projects have been financed by international aid, but such aid is decreasing. Tax reforms initiated in 2012 have resulted in a $35 billion increase in tax revenues for future development, and the government entered an agreement with the World Bank in 2013 to further improve tax administration and collection.[4]

- *Measuring progress.* The consolidation policies do not contain a monitoring and evaluation strategy to track and compare changes over time. Progress indicators are undefined, so there is no way to test claims of success, which compromises the government's transparency and accountability.

The broader question that Colombia's consolidation effort raises is one of governance. The purpose of the consolidation effort is to incorporate formerly abandoned communities into national citizenship. The fundamental challenge is not, however, simply to remove guerrillas and replace them with functioning security, justice, and service provision authorities, which is the basic purpose of the consolidation programs. The fundamental challenge is to shift power away from informal and illicit governance actors, to communities and state authorities who legitimately represent the communities. But power in rural Colombia has long been held by large landowners. The paramilitary movement and some major organized criminal groups emerged from the class of rural, wealthy, informal power brokers who saw their property threatened by guerrillas or found opportunity in narcotrafficking. They have been the main contributors to anti-guerrilla death squads and paramilitaries and the main sources of Colombia's corruption.

Even though the Victims and Land Restitution Law has been implemented vigorously since 2012, the protections it has afforded to victims and returnees have been mainly defensive, and not universally effective. The perpetrators of violence—those who originally displaced the victims from their lands and those who are today targeting the victims whose land has been returned—have generally not been prosecuted for their crimes. Concerns about the influence of paramilitaries and wealthy rural landowners in government remain widespread.

President Santos has recognized that this is a problem. He has aggressively targeted government corruption during his administration by institutionalizing transparency and accountability measures. In 2011, the Colombian Congress passed the Anti-Corruption Act and established the National Moralization Commission, the Secretariat for the Presidency for Transparency, the Economic Transparency Portal, and the National Public Procurement Agency.[5] However, the reforms have been largely ineffective so far. In 2012, Colombia ranked 94th out of 176 countries in Transparency International's Corruption Perception

4. Wesley Tomaselli, "World Bank Signs On to Fix Colombia Tax Collection," *Colombia Reports*, August 6, 2013, http://colombiareports.co/world-bank-signs-on-to-fix-colombia-tax-collection/.

5. Juan Manuel Santos, "Address by the President of the Republic, Juan Manuel Santos, on the High-Level Whistleblowing Mechanism (v. 7)" (speech, Bogotá, Colombia, April 2, 2013), http://www.baselgovernance.org/fileadmin/docs/news/mecanismo_denuncias_de_alto_nivel_7_eng.pdf.

Index, its worst rating in 10 years.[6] And the World Bank's 2012 Worldwide Governance Indicators rated Colombia's progress in corruption control at a low-range score of 46.4 out of 100.[7]

In April 2013, President Santos announced that Colombia would be the first country in the world to implement the High Level Reporting Mechanism (HLRM) developed by the Basel Institute on Governance and the Organization for Economic Cooperation and Development (OECD).[8] The HLRM aims to curb government corruption through comprehensive government-corporate collaboration to encourage immediate reporting of illegal activity and promptly investigate and prosecute bribery of public officials.[9]

President Santos claims the anti-corruption reforms have shown progress, citing statistics that the government could gain 150 billion pesos from ongoing investigations of 150 officials and 42 previous indictments.[10] However, with 10 percent of the current Congress having been impeached for illegal activity, 46 percent of Colombians believe the new policies have had little effect and 80 percent of the public still perceives the government as fundamentally corrupt.[11]

Casanare

By Douglas Farah

Aguazul, Casanare — One wall of the small conference room off the mayor's office in this oil town is lined with the official portraits of more than a dozen past municipal leaders.

"This mayor is in jail, this one is a fugitive from justice, this one was assassinated," said Osman Fuentes, the mayor's private secretary, pointing at the photographs while waiting for his boss to arrive for an interview. "There is not one that is living here as a free man."

6. Herman Gutierrez, "Colombia: Overview of Corruption and Anti-Corruption," Transparency International, March 15, 2013, http://www.transparency.org/files/content/corruptionqas/373_Colombia_Overview_of_corruption_and_anti-corruption.pdf.

7. World Bank, "Worldwide Governance Indicators: Country Data Report for Colombia, 1996–2012," http://info.worldbank.org/governance/wgi/pdf/c47.pdf.

8. Basel Institute on Governance, "President of Colombia Launches the World's First 'High Level Reporting Mechanism', a Concept Developed by the Basel Institute and OECD," news release, April 16, 2013, http://www.baselgovernance.org/fr/french/news-single-view/archive/2013/april/article/president-of-colombia-launches-the-worlds-first-high-level-reporting-mechanism-a-concept-develop/?tx_ttnews%5BbackPid%5D=323&cHash=711451500d.

9. Basel Institute on Governance and OECD, "High-Level Reporting Mechanism in the Context of Public Procurement: Concept Brief (April 2013)," http://www.baselgovernance.org/fileadmin/docs/news/hlrm_concept_note_v0.3_april13.pdf.

10. Santos, "Address by the President of the Republic, Juan Manuel Santos, on the High-Level Whistleblowing Mechanism."

11. Kevin Howlett, "10% of Colombian Congress 'Impeached,'" *Colombian Politics*, March 9, 2013, http://www.colombia-politics.com/congress-black-list/; Gutierrez, "Colombia: Overview of Corruption and Anti-Corruption"; Kevin Howlett, "80% Label Colombia's Politicians 'Corrupt,'" *Colombia Politics*, July 9, 2013, http://www.colombia-politics.com/corruption-in-colombia/.

The fate of the mayors mirrors the fate of the past seven governors of Casanare Department (Province), where Aguazul is located. All were forced to resign either for corruption or for ongoing ties to right-wing paramilitary groups. None served out a full term in office, and the current governor, elected in a special election in June to replace his recently jailed predecessor, has already been publicly linked to past paramilitary activity.

While parts of Colombia are changing at an astonishing rate, many of the remote areas of the country remain like this potentially rich oil and cattle town that was a paramilitary stronghold—weighted down by a history of political violence, corruption, weak state institutions, and parallel power structures with very little to tie it to the capital or the rest of the nation. In this case the power centers are not the local government institutions, but nonstate actors, including paramilitary groups and oil companies, who have far more resources than local governments and often play the role of arbiter among local power factions.

While the National Policy of Territorial Consolidation and Reconstruction will incorporate 140 municipalities by the end of the year, that figure is less than 10 percent of the nation's 1,119 townships. Leaders of many of those townships not included say they don't understand why they are not made part of the program as well, given the significant levels of violence and isolation their towns have suffered.

"We lost a generation to the 'dirty war,'" said Heli Fernando Camacho, the current mayor of Aguazul. "We have lost our institutionality as a town. We have an unemployment rate of 20 percent, despite having oil companies here. We are moving the violence from the countryside to the towns, and the municipal government has little real power. Our future does not look very bright."

The "dirty war" was fought between paramilitary groups, often paid by the cattle ranchers, who own vast tracts of land in the region, and the FARC, who often extorted and kidnapped the ranchers. The paramilitary factions also fought among themselves. With little state presence, the conflicts wreaked havoc on much of the rural countryside, where many of the best ranches now are abandoned or barely worked. The army and police were seldom present.

The difference between the townships in the Consolidation program with significant resources pouring in, and regions like the swath of oil towns in Casanare Province is striking. In the Consolidation areas, the police and military are a permanent presence and all levels of government, while often struggling, are marshaling resources to build roads, developing long-term strategies to activate local economies, and establishing a nascent judicial presence.

In towns across Casanare the municipal governments are struggling to figure out how to move forward from a violent past and the continuing specter of corruption with fewer resources and little tangible support from the state government. The oil companies exercise considerable power but create few long-term jobs or other tangible benefits for the majority of the residents here, in part because historically most of the royalties paid have been siphoned off through corruption schemes.

Government officials agree that the current Consolidation project must continue to expand, as it has from 7 to 58 to 140 municipalities in the past three years. They argue that the size of the program is simply a function of resources and necessary prioritization. The municipalities included in the current program are viewed as the most fragile and most historically neglected. In a country still fighting various insurgencies and criminal threats, there are simply not enough resources to try to do everything at once, the officials say.

Rather, the government is seeking to build a solid foundation in the most neglected and violent regions first, and from there, to build outward to more townships. As more resources become available and those towns "graduate" to less needy status, more towns will be covered. But officials acknowledge that there are no clear criteria for those participating in the program to be moved out and that those towns in the program are likely to remain there for many years to come.

"We understand that what we can do right now is only a little," said Vice Minister of Defense Jorge Bedoya. "We understand that many are frustrated because they do not yet get anything. But decades of abandonment by the state cannot be solved in one four-year administration. We have to start somewhere."[12]

But that branching out is likely a process that will take years. In the meantime a handful of private-sector programs are trying to step into the breach in new and innovative ways. It is at best a small stop-gap series of programs that are trying to build a base of municipal government that can empower grassroots organizations in battered towns in conflict zones to begin the process of constructing responsive governments.

Alberto Ariza is trying to bring about change on a shoestring budget and the deep conviction that the only way for Colombia's marginalized regions to break the cycles of corruption and violence in which they have been trapped for decades is to empower local citizens.

This means restoring real decisionmaking power and accountability to the local municipal governments, along with resources to give the townships a chance to begin to meet many of the pressing needs. Ariza argues forcefully that

12. Comments during the CSIS forum in Bogotá, Colombia, June 17, 2013.

helping municipal governments, rather than nonstate actors, gain popular legitimacy and power to act is the only way to effectively reestablish government control.

"This is where the people feel the government," said Ariza, a lawyer and former government official who is welcomed warmly at each stop on his hectic two-day visit to Casanare. "This is the organic link between the people and the state. If the municipal governments don't work, if they aren't at the center of the government's strategy, then the policy can't work."

With some funding from the oil companies, local governments, and others, Ariza teaches local leaders, chosen by their communities, basic community organizational skills. This begins at the most basic level by explaining how local governments are supposed to work with the provincial and national governments, what they are empowered to do, and what resources they are entitled to under the law. Rather than a top-down approach, Ariza believes the integration process has to begin from the bottom up.

The task was complicated by a law enacted by the Santos administration in 2011 that dramatically changed the way royalty payments on natural resource extraction are made to the municipalities. Much less money flows directly to the municipal coffers, and much more is being directed to the central government and provincial governments. Part of the reason for the change was the notorious corruption traditionally surrounding these payments for oil, gold, gas, and coal extraction on a local level.

"The royalty payments will no longer be used for small local projects that have little impact, much less for the whims of municipal governments or state governments," President Santos said when the law was enacted. "We are implementing a work plan based on the principles of good governance: efficiency, efficacy, transparency and accountability. And one concept will be key to getting the maximum benefit from these resources — coordination."[13]

Local municipal leaders in several towns here said that by taking more than half of their primary income source, the new law had further weakened municipal governments by depriving them of resources necessary to meet basic community needs. But others said it had only cut out a level of corruption that had existed for decades, where mayors and provincial authorities often gave hugely inflated contracts to close friends and family who stole the money and often left the projects either unfinished or unusable.

13. "Colombia tiene nueva ley de regalías," *Energía en Linea*, July 22, 2013, http://www.energiaenlinea.com/index.php?option=com_content&view=article&id=787:colombia-tiene-nueva-ley-de-regalias&catid=68:categoria-noticias-gas-natural&Itemid=537.

But everyone agreed that the coordination among different levels of the state that was to be the cornerstone of the new structure has been slow to materialize or nonexistent. Many here have no clear idea who they are supposed to be coordinating with or how the new system is supposed to prioritize funding proposals from towns and villages dispersed over large regions. A particularly weak link is between the municipal governments themselves, with little history of cooperation among themselves, and among the municipal governments and the provincial governments.

"The basic problem here is that the state is not here," Ariza said as he prepared to teach an all-day seminar to 30 communal leaders from 12 of the outlying hamlets of the town of Paz de Ariporo. "The FARC was the government, the AUC was the government, but the people have never been the government."

The seminar is part of a diploma program that runs over eight weekends, designed to help community leaders be more effective. Ariza and his team spend the time with team-building exercises, videos of TED talks, and lectures on empowering their local townships. Those gathered are broken into smaller working groups to design projects to deal with specific local problems, such as garbage collection, safe public spaces for young people, municipal art projects. The discussions in the groups are lively and sometimes heated as the participants grapple with how to build realistic responses in their hometowns.

José Alfredo Vásquez and his wife, Maricela, who had traveled several hours to attend the seminar from the hamlet of La Libertad, said the seminars were essential to moving forward. Both serve on their village's communal board.

"We are learning many things we didn't know, like how to organize and how to work collectively," Marciela said. "We are learning how to run a municipality, how to run contracts, how to administer projects, how to relate to the state government. It is opening our eyes."

Paz de Ariporo mayor Edgar Bejarano dropped by the seminar to urge those participating to become more active in setting a common agenda. "We are alone in our process of building a new reality," Bejarano said. "We ask you to accompany us, we need to all work together so we have municipal governments that really work."

One of the most common complaints was that oil companies operating in the region (state-owned Ecopetrol, Equion, and Total) have created few permanent jobs yet brought a host of problems. Bejarano said that all the municipalities that have oil, such as his town, remain the poorest because the oil trade drives up the local costs of housing and consumer products while also bringing increased prostitution, petty crime, and congestion.

Along the streets of Paz de Ariporo, nearly identical four-wheel-drive Toyota and Chevrolet pickup trucks crowd the narrow streets, only a few of which are paved. Scores of cheap Chinese-made small motorcycles, many with children perched precariously in front of the driver on the gas tank, dodge the pickups and the enormous potholes filled with rainwater.

The oil companies, according to local residents, bring in their own contractors to do most of the work, driving up prices in the towns while providing few employment opportunities. At the same time, according to Bejarano and others, the oil companies can influence local councilmen, give grants for their pet projects, and undermine the local government.

"Oil is a two-edged sword," Ariza said. "It brings money and conflict. People feel like the land doesn't belong to them anymore. They want to have more say in their destiny."

During one group discussion the issue of citizen participation in municipal government was raised, and one of the participants decried the passivity of the local society in the face of so many challenges. There was an immediate response from others in the group who disputed the notion of passivity. Rather, they argued, for decades many of those who chose to participate were killed with impunity by one side or the other in the conflict. The fear had made it impossible to participate, even if the killings had diminished in recent years.

But participants, most who came from outlying areas that remain far less settled than the towns, warned that the progress was fragile.

"Everything could repeat itself," Vásquez said, referring to the years of violence. "If the government ignores the communities, the violence will return. Right now, the irregular groups are gone, the area is cleaner than it has ever been. Sometimes we see small units of one group or another pass by. People have cell phones, we could help the authorities by letting them know, but we don't really have that level of trust yet. Fear leads people to remain silent."

8 | Social Inclusion

By Robert D. Lamb

As the FARC and other illicit groups recede from territories they had long controlled, the Colombian state has faced the dual imperatives of providing services and treating long-marginalized groups as full citizens. While Colombia is ranked by the World Bank as an upper middle income country, as recently as 2012 about 32.7 percent of the country lived in absolute poverty. That rate represented a decline from 49 percent in 2002, suggesting significant progress over a decade. Progress has also been made in extreme poverty, at 10.4 percent in 2012 (down from 18 percent in 2002), and in a relatively new measure of multidimensional poverty, at 27 percent in 2012 (down from 60 percent in 1997). Rural poverty has long remained significantly higher than urban poverty, with nearly half of the rural population in absolute poverty and nearly a quarter in extreme poverty in 2011. The government has set a national target of 32 percent absolute, 9.5 percent extreme, and 22.5 percent multidimensional poverty by 2014.[1]

Poverty and exclusion do not affect all Colombians equally. The hardest hit are its indigenous and Afro-Colombian communities and internally displaced persons (IDPs). In addition to the psychological effects of losing their homes, IDPs suffer poverty far more than any other group, with 98 percent of IDPs living in absolute poverty and 74 percent in extreme poverty in 2008 (more recent data are not available but the rate has not likely changed much). Given that resources to help IDPs are generally located in cities, while the communities most affected by the violence and coercion that lead to displacement are generally rural, many IDPs never register for government services. About 40 percent of those who do file are denied. Although the rate of displacement has generally declined, upward of 150,000 people were displaced in 2012 and over 55,000 were displaced in first two-thirds of 2013.

Colombia has more than 80 recognized indigenous communities (about 3.4 percent of the total population) and a sizable Afro-Colombian community constituting 11 percent of the population. Both groups have long been disproportionately affected by violence. They represented an estimated 83 percent of all IDPs in Colombia as recently as 2010. Attacks

1. World Bank country data for Colombia, http://data.worldbank.org/country/Colombia; Isabelle Joumard and Juliana London~o Vélez, "Income Inequality and Poverty in Colombia—Part 1: The Role of the Labour Market," OECD Economics Department Working Papers no. 1036, OECD, March 2013, http://dx.doi.org/10.1787/5k487n74s1f1-en.

against Afro-Colombian IDPs and their advocates increased in 2010 and 2011, while violence, land expropriation, and assassinations had put 34 indigenous communities at risk of extermination by around the same time. These and other vulnerable populations are disproportionately affected by natural disasters as well.[2]

Despite progress against poverty overall, inequality remains extremely high in Colombia, as a consequence of violence, high unemployment, high participation in the informal sector, and unequal access to education, among other reasons. About 10 percent of the population earned more than 40 percent of household income, and Colombia's score on the GINI index was 55.9 in 2012, down from 60.7 in 2002 but still among the highest in Latin America.[3]

The UN Office for the Coordination of Humanitarian Affairs (OCHA) projects "a continuation of the current situation, with conflict and drug-related violence and displacement persisting at current trends."

> Armed groups will maintain territorial and social control in localized areas, causing serious humanitarian consequences in the form of displacements and confinements, as well as through killings and threats against community or victim leaders and public officials. The impact of natural disasters is expected to maintain its trend, especially on the most vulnerable populations located in remote areas.[4]

Colombia has made progress on all of these issues over the past decade. But there have also been enough brief reversals in that period that it is not yet clear whether the gains have been sustainably consolidated. In fact, the *Americas Quarterly* Social Inclusion Index showed a slight decline in Colombia's overall ranking since last year, now at ninth out of 16 countries in the hemisphere, due to low rankings in women's poverty, civil rights, and personal empowerment. Compared to other countries in the Americas, it has done reasonably well by a number of other measures, including GDP growth (fifth of 16), social program spending (seventh of 16), women's rights (tied for second), and gay rights (tied for fourth).[5]

But IDPs and Afro-Colombian, indigenous, and rural communities remain among Colombia's most disadvantaged populations, and it pays to see what efforts have been made to reduce their social exclusion.

---

2. UN Office for the Coordination of Humanitarian Affairs (OCHA), "OCHA in 2012 & 2013: Plan and Budget: Colombia," http://www.unocha.org/ocha2012-13/Colombia; Chloe Stirk, *Colombia: Resources for Humanitarian Response and Poverty Reduction* (Bristol, UK: Global Humanitarian Assistance, April 2013), http://www.globalhumanitarianassistance.org/wp-content/uploads/2013/04/Colombia-final-draft.pdf; UNHCR Colombia Mission, "Report of the Special Rapporteur on the Situation of Human Rights and Fundamental Freedoms of Indigenous People," May 25, 2010, http://daccess-dds-ny.un.org/doc/UNDOC/GEN/G10/136/69/PDF/G1013669.pdf?OpenElement.
3. World Bank, "GINI Index," http://data.worldbank.org/indicator/SI.POV.GINI; Joumard and Vélez, "Income Inequality and Poverty in Colombia—Part 1."
4. OCHA, "OCHA in 2012 & 2013: Plan and Budget: Colombia."
5. "The Social Inclusion Index 2013," *Americas Quarterly* (Summer 2013), http://americasquarterly.org/charticles/Social_Inclusion_Index_2013/index.html.

The importance of social inclusion has been formally recognized for more than two decades. Colombia's 1991 constitution recognized the multiethnic and multicultural nature of the Colombian people. Since then, a number of laws, agencies, policies, and initiatives have been implemented to facilitate minority participation in politics and society and to protect at-risk groups from exploitation.

In 1997 the Colombian legislature passed Law 387 declaring a formal right not to be forcibly displaced and a responsibility of the Colombian state to prevent displacement, help victims, and establish social and economic conditions conducive to equality, justice, and peaceful coexistence. It assigned implementation roles to 15 agencies of the state, and a national registry of IDPs was set up.[6] Since then the national legislature has passed more than a dozen decrees and resolutions on specific issues related to displacement, including regulations, new committees, and national plans.[7]

But the Colombian Constitutional Court ruled in 2004 that IDPs were being systematically and unconstitutionally denied the protections and rights granted to them under Law 387, blaming inadequate institutional capacity and financing.[8] The following year, the government committed more than $2 billion over five years to take corrective action and implement new policies. Some progress was made, but in late 2011 the Constitutional Court again ruled that the system for protecting IDPs was still inadequate.[9]

By then, however, President Santos had already signed the most significant law yet to protect victims. The Victims and Land Restitution Law, signed in June 2011, set up a system to return millions of acres of land taken from about 4 million victims of Colombia's conflicts, provide other forms of compensation when restitution was not possible, centralize victims registries, and establish new policies and bodies to implement the law. Implementation of this initiative, unprecedented in its ambition, has proceeded vigorously since 2012. But many returnees have been threatened and killed, prosecutions of those responsible for originally displacing them have been few, and the actions taken to protect returnees have been limited mainly to increased defensive security rather than more significant steps to stem the power of armed actors threatening victims, returnees, and their advocates. In response, the government, security forces, the Attorney General's Office, the Prosecutor General's Office, and the National Protection Unit have established integrated intelligence centers to provide safety measures and draw risk assessment maps in the areas where victims have requested land restitution. The National Protection Unit coordinates and enforces protection provisions for organizations and people whose lives have been threatened and are under elevated risk as a

6. El Congreso de Colombia, "Ley 387 de 1997 (Julio 18)," *Diario Oficial* No. 43.091 de 24 de julio de 1997, http://www.secretariasenado.gov.co/senado/basedoc/ley/1997/ley_0387_1997.html.

7. Brookings-LSE Project on Internal Displacement, "Colombia Laws and Policies on Internal Displacement," http://www.brookings.edu/about/projects/idp/laws-and-policies/Colombia.

8. "Decision No. T-025 of 2004," Colombian Constitutional Court, Bogotá, Colombia, January 22, 2004, http://www.brookings.edu/~/media/Projects/idp/Colombia_T%20025_2004.pdf.

9. "Auto 219 de 2011," Colombian Constitutional Court, Bogotá, Colombia, October 13, 2011, http://www.internal-displacement.org/8025708F004CE90B/(httpDocuments)/DCF82F20962D5239C125796000449F3D/$file/Auto+219,+Octubre+2011.pdf.

result of their rank or activities. Police efforts to target such armed actors are still in the early states.[10]

Also in 2011, the Department for Social Prosperity was created to consolidate most government agencies responsible for making and implementing policies related to poverty reduction, victims compensation, and peace keeping. Related reforms included the establishment of a state Sector for Social Inclusion and Reconciliation, updates to welfare provisions, support to the National Agency for Overcoming Extreme Poverty, and efforts to attract private-sector involvement. Many related projects seem to be progressing, although sufficient data are not yet available to judge them. The land-registry effort has gotten off to a much slower start than hoped (see Chapter 4 on land tenure).[11]

The United States has committed funds to support Colombia's social inclusion policies. For example, it has committed funds for projects to support human rights and the social and economic development of disadvantaged groups, especially Afro-Colombian and indigenous communities and former child soldiers. It is also funding efforts to expand legal agriculture and economic development in former conflict zones and key rural areas.[12]

Still, the U.S. contribution to Colombia's consolidation efforts is declining, and the Colombian government is looking to attract funding partners, including in the private sector, an effort the United States supports. In June 2013, USAID announced a three-year, $3 million partnership with Starbucks Coffee Company to improve coffee yields and livelihoods of farmers in rural Antioquia, Tolima, Huila, and Cauca, including for those affected by coca eradication.[13] A recent partnership between USAID and NewCom is intended to improve Internet access in remote communities, connect farmers to distant markets, provide financial management services, and help in weather forecast adaptation.[14] The Colombian Ministry of Education is set to assume the responsibility of continuing the project after USAID phases out at the end of the year.[15]

In the summer of 2013, farmers across Colombia—later joined by others—in a series of protests across the country began demonstrating their discontent with the pace of reform. Some reforms have already shown progress. Agricultural production is rising, and the Colombian government and the FARC have, in peace talks, successfully negotiated over

---

10. El Congreso de Colombia, "Ley No. 1448 de 10 Jun. 2011," http://www.brookings.edu/~/media/Projects/idp/laws%20and%20policies%20added%20after%202012/Colombia_1448_2011.pdf; Human Rights Watch, *The Risk of Returning Home.*

11. Schwab Foundation for Social Entrepreneurship, *Breaking the Binary: Policy Guide to Scaling Social Innovation* (Geneva: World Economic Forum, April 2013), 19–21, http://www.weforum.org/pdf/schwabfound/PolicyGuide_to_ScalingSocial%20Innovation.pdf.

12. Bureau of Counterterrorism, *Country Reports on Terrorism 2012* (Washington, DC: U.S. Department of State, May 2013), http://www.state.gov/documents/organization/210204.pdf.

13. Craig Russell, "A New Partnership to Support Colombia's Coffee Farmers," *USAID Impact Blog*, August 26, 2013, http://blog.usaid.gov/2013/08/new-partnership-to-support-colombias-coffee-farmers.

14. USAID, "USAID and NewCom Partner to Increase Broadband Access in the Americas," June 18, 2013, http://www.usaid.gov/news-information/press-releases/usaid-and-newcom-partner-increase-broadband-access-americas.

15. USAID, "USAID Forward Progress Report 2013," http://www.usaid.gov/sites/default/files/documents/1868/2013-usaid-forward-report.pdf.

land reform. But as the Colombian peso has strengthened over the past decade, domestic agriculture and industry have become less competitive. And rural areas remain significantly worse off than urban areas in terms of poverty, infrastructure, services, and other measures. As a result, rural discontent remains high, especially since expectations were raised when the Victims Law was passed.[16]

It is clear, therefore, that many challenges to social inclusion remain. But the main one might simply be institutionalizing and implementing the policies already in place. Meeting raised expectations will take significant effort and apparently a longer time than many Colombians want to wait.

16. Andres Schipani, "Colombia grapples with aftermath of protests by farmers," FT.com, September 22, 2013, http://www.ft.com/intl/cms/s/0/3bd55e64-21e4-11e3-9b55-00144feab7de.html#axzz2iJnd0Ys1.

9 Recommendations and Conclusions

By Carl Meacham

Given this report's exploration of the current state of Colombia's ongoing conflict and the challenges the government and country will continue to face going forward, the authors propose the following recommendations.

The U.S.-Colombia strategic partnership should continue for the foreseeable future—even if the ongoing peace process proves successful in formally ending the principal conflict and resolving the several outstanding issues on its agenda.

The political implications of losing influence in Colombia would be significant. Damage to that relationship could imply losing a key ally who has consistently demonstrated support for policies key to U.S. interests—both in the region and around the world.

But furthering their cooperation, the U.S. and Colombian governments must become flexible and agile in dealing with the shifting security challenges the two will face in Colombia moving forward. The recent shifts in the nature of the conflict are largely the reflection of the success of the joint strategy of dismantling the major existential threats to the state—but maintaining the current positive trends will require a constant reevaluation of the national strategy and goals, as well as of resource allocation.

In that vein, the following issues will likely emerge as central to the two countries' partnership in the future: land restitution; offensive action against nonguerrilla perpetrators of violence; support for the Colombian judiciary; resource allocation for internally displaced persons; protection for the country's indigenous communities and other vulnerable groups; and the clearing of nonstate armed actors from areas of illicit resource extraction.

- *Land Restitution:* The issue of land restitution must remain among the top priorities of the partnership. The recent progress has given the government some proverbial breathing room, with an opportunity to establish a positive state presence. Still, the issue has the real potential to develop into a fatal bottleneck. Land disputes deeply affect the Colombian population, and are often a primary driver of rural violence. Efforts to resolve this complex and thorny problem must be accelerated, and U.S. aid in this field should ideally focus on providing technological support to these efforts. While the horizon for measuring success remains, at best, several years off, the more robust the effort, the more credible the overall strategy becomes.

- *Nonguerrilla Perpetrators of Violence:* Should the conflict with armed guerrilla forces wind down, the greatest threat to both social inclusion and government consolidation will likely be the continued impunity of the powerful nonguerrilla landholders whose private security details continue to threaten and attack vulnerable minorities, internally displaced persons (IDPs), and recently victims who have returned to their land. Whether these groups are referred to as demobilized paramilitaries, BACRIM, or simply power brokers protecting their perceived interests, their continued impunity demonstrates not only that the state does not have a monopoly on violence—even despite the departure of guerrillas—but also that the state is unwilling and/or unable to live up to is promises to treat the excluded and vulnerable as citizens worthy of state protection. Moving forward, the state needs to build its capacity to pursue, investigate, prosecute, and (if necessary) do battle against those who continue to perpetrate violence.
- *The Colombian Judiciary:* The judiciary has, without a doubt, come a long way since the 1990s. That said, the courts continue to suffer from understaffing, rendering them incapable of keeping up with the need to prosecute perpetrators of crimes and with the demand for specialized legal services as land and property rights issues emerge and develop. Support for paralegal training and scholarships for law school students might be useful steps in addresses these issues in the medium term, building judicial capacity to benefit the country in coming years.
- *Internally Displaced Persons (IDPs):* The deficiency of resources for IDPs continues to hamper the process of reintegrating these people into their communities of origin. Regional IDP centers should be set up in more remote areas—perhaps in tandem with other government offices—so that IDPs need not travel long distances to register for and receive the services provided for them. The U.S. and Colombian governments should work together to institutionalize the changes that have already been made and ensure the institutions and personnel that work to better this issue are adequately trained and financially supported.
- *Indigenous and Vulnerable Groups:* Indigenous communities and other vulnerable groups—among them women and Afro-Colombians—remain disproportionately affected by the conflict and its implications—in particular by violence and land expropriation. Many Afro-Colombian and indigenous communities, especially those seeking to preserve their way of life, remain too poor to adequately represent themselves before the courts or protect themselves from all sides of the conflict. Every effort should be made to ensure the protection of their traditional lands, ensuring that title to their lands is not improperly awarded to other claimants—and to provide legal services and other forms of support to improve their access to the judicial system.

- *Illicit Resource Extraction:* Efforts should focus, as a military priority, on the clearing of nonstate armed actors from areas of illicit extraction of minerals and other resources. The ability of these groups to access and sell coltan, gold, emeralds, and other minerals both deprives the state of revenue and has served as an economic lifeline for irregular groups that feed into the nation's violence. Illegal mining—when carried out by such armed groups—offers a stream of revenue to these actors, and carries few of the risks of being involved in the production and trade of cocaine. The issue must be addressed if the groups are to be deprived of the financial resources they need to continue their operations.

It is also imperative that the Colombian government take on a number of initiatives of its own, including: an effective public messaging campaign to alter continued perceptions that the country remains at war; and a monitoring and evaluation framework, to keep track of whether and to what extent progress is being made in the consolidation programs already in place.

Appendix: CSIS Americas Program Experts Workshop Participants

Roberto Angulo, *Director, Ingreso Social, Departamento para la Prosperidad Social*

Alberto Ariza, *Universidad Sergio Arboleda*

Álvaro Balcázar, *Coordinador General, Plan de Consolidación Integral de la Macarena*

Giovanni Barbosa, *Raven Pipeline Company*

Jorge Enrique Bedoya Vizcaya, *Viceministro de Defensa para las Políticas y Asuntos Internacionales*

Juan Carlos Betancur, *Magistrado Auxiliar, Consejo Superior, Despacho del Magistrado Néstor Raúl Correa, Sala Administrativa, Consejo Superior de la Judicatura*

Germán Chamorro, *Director, Unidad de Consolidación Territorial*

Fernando Cuervo, *Presidente, Corporación Nuevo Arco Iris*

Douglas Farah, *Senior Associate, Americas Program, Center for Strategic and International Studies*

Ana María Ibáñez, *Directora, Centro de Estudios Sobre Desarrollo Económico (CEDE), Universidad de los Andes*

Mauricio Ibáñez, *Coordinador del Fondo Local de Alianza Estratégicas para la Prosperidad Social, ACDI*

Luis Gallo, *Director General, Banca de Inversión Social*

Tulia Inés Gómez, *Centro de Estudios Estratégicos Latinoamericanos (CEELAT)*

María Victoria Llorente, *Directora, Fundación Ideas para la Paz*

Carl Meacham, Director, *Americas Program, Center for Strategic and International Studies*

Rafael Mejía López, *Presidente, Sociedad de Agricultores*

Jenny Molina, *Centro de Estudios Estratégicos Latinoamericanos (CEELAT)*

María Eugenia Pinto, *Unidad de Consolidación Territorial*

Alejandro Reyes, *Asesor, Ministry of Agriculture and Rural Development*

Pablo Reyes, *Presidente, Centro de Estudios Estratégicos Latinoamericanos (CEELAT)*

Ángela Riaño, *Directora de Comunicaciones, regiones Colombia, Venezuela, y el Caribe, Arcos Dorados*

María Rueda, *Centro de Estudios Estratégicos Latinoamericanos (CEELAT)*

Valeria Saldarriaga, *Unidad de Consolidación Territorial*

Evelyn Shoettlaender, *Instituto de Planificación y Promoción de Soluciones Energéticas para las Zonas No Interconectadas (IPSE)*

Gilberto Toro Giraldo, *Director Ejecutivo Federación Colombiana de Municipios*

Gabriel Turriago, *Coordinator, United Nations Development Program*

About the Authors

Carl Meacham is director of the CSIS Americas Program. He joined CSIS from the Senate Foreign Relations Committee (SFRC), where he served on the professional staff for Senator Richard Lugar (R-IN) for over a decade. He served as the senior adviser for Latin America and the Caribbean on the committee, the most senior Republican Senate staff position for this region. In that capacity, he traveled extensively to the region to work with foreign governments, private-sector organizations, and civil society groups. He was also responsible for managing the committee's relationship with the State Department regarding the Western Hemisphere and overseeing its $2 billion budget. Before he joined SFRC, Meacham worked on the staff of two Democratic senators. Prior to his Senate work, he served at the Department of Commerce as special assistant to the deputy secretary, at the Cuban Affairs Bureau of the Department of State, and at the U.S. embassy in Madrid. Meacham is a native speaker of Spanish and was partly raised in Chile, his mother's country of origin. He received his BA from the University at Albany, State University of New York, and holds MA degrees from American University and Columbia University.

Douglas Farah is a senior associate of the Americas Program at CSIS and president at IBI Consultants LLC. He is an expert on transnational criminal organizations, insurgencies, ungoverned spaces, illicit money flows, and resource exploitation in Latin America. In recent years he has written extensively about Iran's growing influence in Latin America, the Bolivarian revolution, and transnational criminal and terrorist networks in the region. From 1985 to 2005 he worked as a journalist, primarily as a foreign correspondent and investigative reporter for the *Washington Post*. In addition to several postings in Latin America, he served as West Africa bureau chief, international investigative correspondent, and a member of the investigative unit. Since leaving the *Post* in 2004, Mr. Farah has worked as a consultant to the U.S. government on national intelligence reform, nonstate armed actors, critical infrastructure protection, criminal-terrorist pipelines, bulk cash smuggling to Mexico, and other topics. He has also worked as a consultant with the World Bank, the Rand Corporation, the Woodrow Wilson International Center for Scholars, and other organizations. He is a frequent lecturer to U.S. military institutions on the FARC and other Latin American insurgencies, and he has testified before Congress on numerous occasions. Mr. Farah is the author of two books: *Blood from Stones: The Secret Financial Network of Terror* (Broadway, 2004) and *Merchant of Death: Money, Guns, Planes and the Man Who Makes War Possible* (Wiley, 2007). He appears regularly in the national and international media and has been published in more than a dozen journals and magazines.

Robert D. Lamb is a senior fellow and director of the Program on Crisis, Conflict and Cooperation at CSIS and a research scholar at the Center for International and Security Studies at the University of Maryland. Dr. Lamb studies governance and development amid conflict, with an emphasis on hybrid political systems and complex crises. He has presented his work to policymakers and experts throughout the United States and in Afghanistan, Colombia, France, Germany, Greece, India, Korea, Pakistan, Romania, Russia, Sweden, and the United Kingdom. A former Defense Department strategist, he has developed tools to help policymakers pay more attention to local governance and informal systems in places that terrorist, criminal, and insurgent networks use as safe havens. As a doctoral candidate, he spent a year in Colombia developing new methods for studying gang governance, violence, and legitimacy in the stateless slums of Medellín, then joined CSIS as a visiting scholar after returning to Washington. He earned a PhD in policy studies from the University of Maryland School of Public Policy in a program combining security, economics, and ethics. He received a BA in interdisciplinary studies from Gettysburg College, spent half a year in Nicaragua with a microdevelopment project, then worked for nine years as an editor and journalist, winning a National Press Club award in 2001, before changing careers after 9/11.

www.ingramcontent.com/pod-product-compliance
Ingram Content Group UK Ltd.
Pitfield, Milton Keynes, MK11 3LW, UK
UKHW051418150926
475561UK00005B/240

9 781442 228